COMMERCIALISATION IN CENTRAL AND EAST EUROPEAN SHIPPING

"They shot Jan in the belly. On December 18, 1970, they shot Jan in his bellyful of pork and cabbage. The police of the People's Republic of Poland shot, along with other workers, the naval construction engineer, employee of the publicity department, trade-union and Communist League member Jan Ludkowski, aged forty-three, in his belly, then full of the pork, and carawayed cabbage that had been dished out to upward of two thousand striking workers in the canteen of the Lenin Shipyard. Just in time, just before the shipyard was cordoned off by the police, Maria Kuczorra, who was in charge of provisioning the shipyard canteen, had managed to divert to the shipyard a truckload of cabbage intended for the army. Deep-frozen pork ribs were already on hand. And there has never been any shortage of caraway seed in Poland. He died instantly."

Günter Grass, *The Flounder* 1977

Business 06/03

SEVEN DAY LOAN
This book is to be returned on
or before the date stamped below

3 0 SEP 2003

2 3 FEB 2004

1 2 MAR 2004

3 1 MAR 2004

2 0 APR 2004

UNIVERSITY OF PLYMOUTH

PLYMOUTH LIBRARY
Tel: (01752) 232323
This book is subject to recall if required by another reader
Books may be renewed by phone
CHARGES WILL BE MADE FOR OVERDUE BOOKS

Commercialisation in Central and East European Shipping

MICHAEL ROE
Institute of Marine Studies
University of Plymouth

Ashgate

Aldershot • Brookfield USA • Singapore • Sydney

Published by
Ashgate Publishing Limited
Gower House
Croft Road
Aldershot
Hants GU11 3HR
England

Ashgate Publishing Company
Old Post Road
Brookfield
Vermont 05036
USA

British Library Cataloguing in Publication Data
Roe, Michael, 1954-
    Commercialisation in central and east European Shipping.-
    (Plymouth studies in contemporary shipping)
    1. Shipping - Poland 2. Shipping - Government policy - Poland
    3. Shipping - Economic aspects - Poland
    I. Title
    387.5 ' 09438 ' 09049

Library of Congress Catalog Card Number: 98-70980

ISBN 1 84014 170 0 ✓

Printed and bound by Athenaeum Press, Ltd.,
Gateshead, Tyne & Wear.

Contents

The ancillary industries

Acknowledgements

So how do you acknowledge all the help given in producing a text like this one? Whilst not being easy, I will do my best to pick out those who contributed most. As is normal practice, to those I leave out without cause, my humblest apologies.

The European Commission, through the Phare (ACE) Programme, which provided the funding for the three trips to Poland during 1996 and 1997, needs to be thanked simply for enabling the research to take place. Despite their continued insistence upon using ECUs for all transactions even though banks in Plymouth have hardly yet moved away from the one pound note, the Phare offices in Brussels have accommodated the rather curious structure to the research without complaint.

Clearly all those interviewed in the Polish maritime sector and listed in the back of this book deserve a mention. Without them there would be little here to read. My heartfelt thanks also goes to Janusz Zurek at the University of Gdańsk who provided such a warm welcome and an academic base for the year it took to gather the material. My other close contacts from Poland also deserve a mention - in particular Magdalena Zalińska, Aleksandra Wrona and Agnieszka Ziemba. Without their help, access to the state Ministry in Warsaw would have been impossible and my ability to pronounce Świnoujście would have remained at the level of abysmal. As it is, it has risen to the dizzy heights of shocking.

I should also thank the publishers of "The Flounder", Martin Secker and Warburg, who have given me permission to quote from Günter Grass's 1977 novel. In truth I feel that it is really the author that I should be thanking, but due to the complexities of the publishing system that exist, this is rather more difficult than it might seem. For anyone with a true interest in Poland, and particularly the area around Gdańsk where the maritime sector is centred, there is no better source of atmosphere than the books by Grass and in particular, "The Tin Drum", "The Flounder", "Cat and Mouse" and "The Call of the Toad" which together trace the region's development from the early twentieth century, through the occupation by the Germans and the free city of Danzig, to today's Gdańsk.

Finally I need to thank that small group of people who feature in the acknowledgements of everything I write - and with some reason. Marie Bendell at the Institute of Marine Studies, who remains a remarkable woman both in terms of her organisational abilities and the care she takes of me. I could ask for no-one better. And Liz, Joe and Siân, at home in Yelverton, who put up with an endless succession of stories about Poland, ships and football. Without their support and humour none of it would be worthwhile.

Michael Roe, Plymouth
December 12th, 1997.

Introduction

This text attempts to analyse the rapidly changing face of the Polish maritime sector as the developments in the political, economic and social climate of the late 1980s and the 1990s begin to bite and have an effect upon the region of East Europe. By the nature of the changes which have occurred throughout the former CMEA countries, this is a difficult, if not nearly impossible process as the pace of change commonly is faster than any commentator can write and publish, and the types of changes taking place are often unpredictable both in their nature and their outcomes.

Despite these overwhelming odds it is felt that this text is still a worthwhile venture in documenting the change so far - at the end of 1997 - so that those interested in the region and the economic sector will have some material upon which to base future judgements and to assess the decisions made during these dynamic years.

The text is divided into a number of rather artificial sections - artificial because the maritime industry is not easily separated into operators, ports and ancillary/support businesses as each is interdependent upon the other. However, this division does give the text some structure and may help to guide the reader through the industry as a whole and to understand and interpret the changes that are and continue to be taking place.

The research upon which the discussion was based was funded through the European Union ACE (Phare) programme as noted elsewhere and builds upon a long standing programme of research activity conducted by the Institute of Marine Studies at the University of Plymouth which covers the period in East Europe from the early 1980s onwards. Unlike many new research initiatives, it thus benefits from practical and tangible research which was taking place before the fundamental effects of "perestroika" and "glasnost" were felt in the CMEA region and the researchers involved thus have a broader and more accurate picture of the difficulties facing the region and sector. Much of this research is featured in a large number of publications listed at the end of the text (21,22,23,68,69). Other institutes within the region have also collaborated within this research programme and developed their own independent work building upon previous studies which the reader might like to follow up (3,4,24,55,56,57,71,78,79,80,81).

Poland is not an easy country within which to conduct research, not because of an unfriendly attitude but simply because custom and tradition requires a number of visits to develop trust and openness. The research outlined here is thus of considerable significance in that it is a product of long term relationships in dealing with a naturally, and understandably confidential business activity. It is hoped that the reader will appreciate these factors when using the text. If further illumination is needed on any issue within the research remit, then the author would be delighted to provide this; you are advised to contact him at the University of Plymouth.

Poland's Recent History and the Maritime Sector

Introduction

Largely as a result of its spatial location adjacent to the Former Soviet Union, Poland's post-war history and development has been fundamentally influenced by the rise and subsequent fall of Communism in the region. Poland emerged from the second world war in 1945, physically destroyed but with a spirit of independence that was eliminated by the invasion of influence and control by the Soviet Union who, although on the face of it encouraged and permitted an independent Poland to exist, in fact dominated the territory in terms of economy, politics and social fabric through a complex and at times subtle system of price and currency controls, armed forces and secret police.

It wasn't until the 1970s before any significant signs of change began to emerge when the industrial community in Poland began to attempt to exercise their political strength only to be defeated once again through armed conflict and a period of martial law. However the seeds of independence had been planted and looking back, it is now possible to see that the social, political and economic changes that have swept through Eastern Europe as a whole since the mid 1980s began in Poland some 10 - 15 years earlier in the battles commencing in the shipyards of Gdańsk (2, 20).

It is not our purpose here to describe in any detail the political history of Poland even though there are undoubtedly times when the relationship between the shipping industry and political developments are very close - this is true in all countries. Where the two are closely interrelated, then these relationships will be pointed out and analysed. However, to have any appreciation of the current state of any industrial or commercial sector in

3

Eastern Europe today, one has to understand the most recent of developments and the context within which the various enterprises now have to operate.

Undoubtedly, the most radical and long lasting of the reforms which have continued to affect Poland to this day began in 1989 with the commencement of the Solidarity government of Tadeusz Mazowiecki with that most influential of Deputy Prime Ministers, Leszek Bałcerowicz. The reforms proposed by the team working under the latter were implemented in January 1990 in an attempt to address the problems inherited from 40 years of Communist rule.

The problems facing the new administration were substantial and complex but can be summarised following the work of Sachs (1993) (71) as follows;

(1) The Polish economy lagged far behind the income and productivity levels of all Western European countries. This was reflected in a number of ways including examples of low consumption of consumer durables, few telephones, few of which worked properly, and few private cars.

(2) Poland was highly industrialised as a deliberate consequence of the Communist period of rule which aimed to build security and prosperity through the development of heavy industry leading in turn to the neglect of lighter (and more modern) industrial sectors and the service sector. The latter, in Sachs (1993) opinion, were starved of resources due to the deliberate direction of investment into the heavy industrial sectors. In 1989, some 61% of all output in Poland was from heavy industry - around twice the OECD rate at that time. The service sector lacked any reasonable amount of activity orientated towards distribution, wholesaling, retailing, catering, finance and public administration. There simply were very few banks, transport providers, plumbers, shops, restaurants etc., and those that there were, were dominated by few or a single state owned provider. In the shipping sector, for example, there was one state owned ships' agency, one chartering agency and one ship chandlers (80).

(3) The existence of a large peasant agriculture sector with low incomes and predominantly still private in ownership, despite numerous attempts to nationalise it by the state. As such it was a highly politically motivated group. Some 29% of employment and 13% of GDP was in the agricultural sector - the highest in Europe.

(4) The economy otherwise was predominantly state owned and to a far greater degree than any other country in Eastern Europe barring the Former Soviet Union. In fact almost 100% of all Polish industry and commerce was

state owned with around 3000 state enterprises. There had been no attempts to privatise and these state companies operated within a market dominated by other state companies or by themselves alone. This is of major significance in terms of economic restructuring generally, and the shipping industry in particular, as we shall see later (67).

(5) International trade was predominantly towards the Former Soviet Union and its colleagues in the CMEA (Council for Mutual Economic Assistance). This was a deliberate result of Soviet dominated trade policies aimed at linking the satellite states of the CMEA into its own economy for political and economic purposes. This resulted in a predominance of soft currency trade (i.e. unconvertible, commonly rouble based) and inevitably a desperate need to acquire hard currency through other means such as tourism, international trucking, prostitution and shipping. The effect of this on the latter's activities and need for restructuring following the transformation of the 1980/1990s, will be discussed later.

(6) Following the primary CMEA principle of economies of scale, Poland was dominated by large enterprises by the late 1980s, with very few small and medium sized companies either privately or state owned. No attempts had been made to develop any semblance of competition in any sector - including commercial shipping - and each sizeable state firm tended to encompass all the activities that had any sort of relationship to the core of the industry thus avoiding the necessity to rely upon other state enterprises whose consistency of delivery was commonly questionable. Thus for example, the single, state owned, bulk shipping company - PZM - would not only operate ships but would also run hostels, holiday camps and retail outlets for its employees amongst many other activities (80).

(7) Income and wealth were very evenly spread, apart from the very few Communist favoured party leaders. As Sachs emphasises, by the late 1980s almost everyone in Poland was poor. This had one beneficial effect in that the moral, ethical and political conditions for market based changes were as ideal as they could be.

It was this set of problems that faced the transformation of Poland during the 1980 - mid 1990s period and the shipping sector was not exempt from these issues and certainly has not been exempt from the transformation of the economy and social structure that has followed.

During 1990, Poland continued to stumble into deep recession largely as a consequence of the government's attempts to create a free market economy from nothing, assisted by aid from the IMF, US government and the (then)

European Community. In particular, and as a direct consequence of the need to readjust prices to realistic levels from those artificially established and maintained by the Communist regime throughout the CMEA and in Poland itself, GDP fell by 11.6% in 1990 and again by 7% in 1991 and unemployment rose rapidly from 0% of the workforce in 1988, to 6% in 1990 and again to 16% in 1994 (7, 53, 54).

Meanwhile, Jaruzelski had resigned in late 1990 as President of Poland allowing the first free elections to take place. The Solidarity leader Lech Walésa won easily and set into motion accelerated reforms with the results in terms of the economy, that we have already seen.

Much change has taken place since then and the reforms in many cases have hardly begun or certainly had little time to have effect (5, 8, 16, 17, 18). Poland's economy in Eastern Europe was the first to show any sign of recovery with a 5% growth of GDP in 1993 assisted by the agreements reached with debtors over external repayments. Political instability followed during the period of 1990 - 3 but the process of reform continued. This has been sustained despite the victory of the ex-Communist Party in 1993 and 1995 in the Parliamentary and Presidential elections and a subsequent reversal in 1997. Economic conditions continue to improve overall, but with indications of a growing division in society between those who are increasingly reaping rewards and those left behind. GDP is estimated to have grown by 5% in 1994, 7% in 1995, a similar amount again in 1996 and with a further increase in 1997. Industrial production is rising steadily (e.g. 14% in the first quarter of 1995) and export revenues rose by 23% in 1995 over 1994. Inflation is largely curbed compared with the excesses of 1990, although interest rates remain high (10, 13, 76).

The maritime sector

In this book, the results of a year long research study of the Polish maritime sector are detailed, funded through the resources of the ACE (Phare) Programme of the European Union. The aim is not simply to trace the transformation that has taken place in Poland as a whole, but more specifically to present the results from the period of research in assessing the success in 1996/1997 of the state run shipping, ports and ancillary sector to adapt and change in the light of the substantial political, social and economic pressures that have been recognised. At the time of the commencement of the transformation, the entire maritime industry was owned, managed and organised by a series of state monopolies whose main functions fitted into those of all such organisations in the old regimes of Eastern Europe - essentially to provide the services needed economically (e.g. run ports, ships,

Figure 1
Organisation of the Polish Maritime Sector, 1989

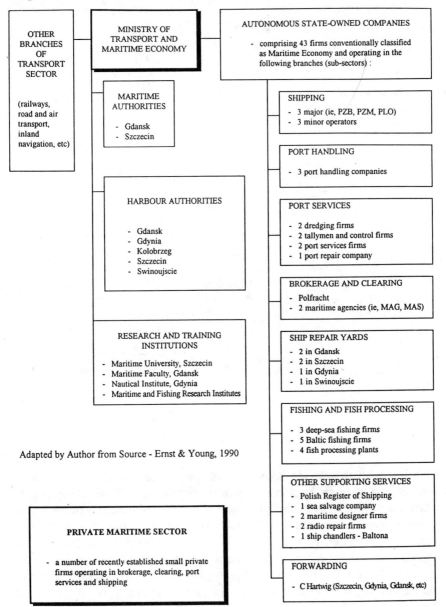

| OTHER BRANCHES OF TRANSPORT SECTOR | MINISTRY OF TRANSPORT AND MARITIME ECONOMY | AUTONOMOUS STATE-OWNED COMPANIES |

OTHER BRANCHES OF TRANSPORT SECTOR

(railways, road and air transport, inland navigation, etc)

MINISTRY OF TRANSPORT AND MARITIME ECONOMY

AUTONOMOUS STATE-OWNED COMPANIES

- comprising 43 firms conventionally classified as Maritime Economy and operating in the following branches (sub-sectors):

MARITIME AUTHORITIES

- Gdansk
- Szczecin

SHIPPING

- 3 major (ie, PZB, PZM, PLO)
- 3 minor operators

PORT HANDLING

- 3 port handling companies

HARBOUR AUTHORITIES

- Gdansk
- Gdynia
- Kolobrzeg
- Szczecin
- Swinoujscie

PORT SERVICES

- 2 dredging firms
- 2 tallymen and control firms
- 2 port services firms
- 1 port repair company

BROKERAGE AND CLEARING

- Polfracht
- 2 maritime agencies (ie, MAG, MAS)

RESEARCH AND TRAINING INSTITUTIONS

- Maritime University, Szczecin
- Maritime Faculty, Gdansk
- Nautical Institute, Gdynia
- Maritime and Fishing Research Institutes

SHIP REPAIR YARDS

- 2 in Gdansk
- 2 in Szczecin
- 1 in Gdynia
- 1 in Swinoujscie

Adapted by Author from Source - Ernst & Young, 1990

FISHING AND FISH PROCESSING

- 3 deep-sea fishing firms
- 5 Baltic fishing firms
- 4 fish processing plants

OTHER SUPPORTING SERVICES

- Polish Register of Shipping
- 1 sea salvage company
- 2 maritime designer firms
- 2 radio repair firms
- 1 ship chandlers - Baltona

PRIVATE MARITIME SECTOR

- a number of recently established small private firms operating in brokerage, clearing, port services and shipping

FORWARDING

- C Hartwig (Szczecin, Gdynia, Gdansk, etc)

Figure 2
Maritime Poland

Source: Author

agencies etc.); to provide some sort of covert state activity in terms of security, and to earn hard currency or restrict its expenditure wherever and whenever possible (see Figure 1). A map of the general locations of the Polish maritime sector can be found in Figure 2. The shipping sector was particularly adept at the latter two functions in that it commonly traded on the international market place, earning hard currency on the crosstrades in the process. The result of this combination of objectives, placed in the context of the Communist led regime and in an international framework of the Soviet dominated CMEA, was in some ways a unique industry in Poland - large state monopolies, with extensive non economic remits, operating in many cases extensively in the free markets of the western world (24,27,45). It is the aim of this text to assess the level of adaptation achieved to the demands of the

8

free market placed upon the sector by the transformations that have occurred in the 1980s and 1990s and this was planned to be achieved by spending extended periods of time with the survivors of the state run enterprises that once dominated and controlled the sector. These state enterprises included the major players detailed below some of which remain, even by late 1997, largely state owned despite considerable publicity about moves towards the establishment of a private maritime market and some notable changes in services provided (41). The functions indicated below summarise their activities before the major changes which have taken place. More details of these functions can be found in the specific sections :

Polska Żegluga Morska (PZM)	- predominantly bulk shipping
Polska Żegluga Bałtycka (PZB)	- predominantly ferry shipping
Polskie Linie Oceaniczne (PLO)	- predominantly liner shipping
POL Levant	- general cargo ship operator
EuroAfrica Linie	- liner and ferry operator
Morska Agencja Gdynia (MAG)	- ships' agency, brokers, consultants, liner agents, P and I representatives
Polfracht	- shipbroking/chartering
Port of Gdańsk	- port management and operation
Port of Gdynia	- port management and operation
Port of Szczecin/Świnoujście	- port management and operation
C Hartwig Gdynia	- international forwarders
C Hartwig Szczecin	- international forwarders
Morska Agencja Szczecin	- ship and port agents, shipbrokers, liner and average agents
Polsteam Tankers Ltd	- bulk tanker operators
Baltona FTC	- ships' suppliers

The text that follows will examine each of these organisations in some detail, and along with information and opinion gained from discussion with experts and policy-makers at the Institute of Maritime Studies and Seaborne Trade, University of Gdańsk and the Ministry of Marine Economy in Warsaw (55). Each will be assessed as they looked during the period from October 1996 to December 1997. In particular, they will be examined for real evidence of structural change and signs of commercialisation as they adapt to the continued and pressing need to privatise in the new free market that is dominating in Poland generally and beginning to impact upon the maritime market more specifically.

Polskie Linie Oceanicze (Polish Ocean Lines)

Introduction

This section will concentrate on the situation in the troubled state operator Polskie Linie Oceanizne - otherwise known as Polish Ocean Lines or POL, but will more specifically consider one of the new companies that has emerged from the parent, in this case POL Levant. Other new subsidiaries will be discussed along the way - e.g. POL America, Polcontainer etc. as the situation dictates. POL Levant is one of the new companies emerging from the restructuring of the Polish liner industry since the reformation that took place in the Polish economy from the late 1980s and as such presents one of the more interesting case studies of change that can be found in the Polish maritime sector. The current situation, in late 1997, cannot be understood without a brief review of the parent company of Polish Ocean Lines (Polskie Linie Oceanizne) and from this, the origins of POL Levant itself.

POL originated in 1920 as Gdynia-America Line, progressing after the end of the second world war as Polish Ocean Lines and from then on as a state owned operator. POL was always a large ship operator even by world standards with, for some years, over 250 vessels. In the 1950 -1990 period it provided extensive liner and general cargo services for the Polish economy in terms of both imports and exports, but in addition, and possibly even more so, it was a hard currency earner and conserver as all major expenditure could be in local (złoty) unconvertible currency and thus avoiding the need to use up scarce and valuable convertible currency reserves. The consequence of this was that much of Polish industry (and other CMEA countries) was forced to use it regardless of quality of service and could use alternative operators only with specific central state approval through the Ministry. This was rarely given except in times of emergency or over demand and when no other possibility existed. All trading contracts were controlled by the state owned Foreign Trade Organisations (FTOs) who would conclude international trading contracts on conditions that guaranteed the state operator control of the transport of the freight. One consequence of all this was that POL prospered and by the 1970s, at the peak of its power, had reached the size of 11000 employees and 178 ships. To place this in perspective and to illustrate the change that has take place in the Polish shipping industry, by 1997 there were only around 6500 staff (seafarers and shore staff) and 44 ships located in the subsidiary firms analysed below. However, the significance that the organisation retains in the Polish maritime sector is emphasised by the 500000 DWT that this ship ownership represents, which carried in 1996 some 4.3m tonnes of cargo of which only half was Polish trade.

In addition to the central state control noted above, all Polish shipping was expected to search out crosstrade work wherever possible paid for in hard currency, which could then be paid into state funds to support any type of state activity. This might include shipping investment, but traditionally the shipping industry was under funded compared with its earning capabilities and record. The shipping companies themselves, including POL had no rights to retain income and were forced to declare and hand over all income to the state. On most occasions this was the case.

The main criterion of success in the pre revolution days was one of US$ generated per złoty spent. The result was that commonly, cargo was carried even at a loss as long as payment was in dollars and in turn this meant that POL provided extensive world-wide services far beyond those that might be normally expected from an operator in that market place and location. Commonly, official and black market $/złoty exchange rates were ignored and earnings per złoty artificially inflated to gain central credibility and to make the company look successful and profitable from the outside. An example of this whole approach to operating was that POL ships were forced commonly to bunker in Poland (or other CMEA locations) regardless of lengthy extra ballast voyages.

In 1986, for reasons that seem to be lost in the mists of time, the Ministry decided to reconsolidate POL back into a single organisation located at a single location in Gdynia - against much of the expressed desire of the divisions within the company. The effect of this was the series of economic and financial disasters that have subsequently hit POL up until the present time stemming from the inadequate and ill designed management structure that was imposed and from a succession of dubious internal transfers of hard currency between different departments of the newly structured company in a vain attempt to keep it financially afloat. Problems were exacerbated by the floating of the złoty coupled within the general economic decline of Polish trade in the early 1990s, the redirection of previously guaranteed traffic and the introduction of accurate and acceptable accounting procedures. One specific example of the problems stemmed from the imposition under the Bałerowicz regime of new taxation laws that included additional salary taxes payable only by state owned companies - of which POL was one. The result of this was a loss of talented staff to privatised or semi-privatised organisations who could afford to offer more pay, and thus a further problem for POL in its attempts to reform and survive.

A major company structural response to all these problems led eventually to the situation that now exists including the emergence and development of POL Levant (30). In 1991, the first of the newly devised independent and legally (if not wholly) privatised companies was created in EuroAfrica. Shares in the former Szczecin branch of POL were offered to private investors and companies thus creating a new private shipping company with all the benefits (e.g. no salary tax) that this brings.

POL Levant

POL Levant was the third separate company to be formed of a series which continues to this day with POL-SEAL, Polcontainer and others some of which are rather more independent of the parent (POL) company. POL Levant emerged on 1st May 1993 with an initial objective of revitalising its market activities through avoidance of public sector taxation regimes and attracting the best quality employees through relocation in the private sector. Political acceptability was also a major stimulus at this time. POL Levant was established with six vessels chartered from the parent company POL and from POL America. These vessels were employed on the existing Mediterranean services of POL, both conventional and ro-ro and which have with some adaptation and development, continued to this day. By the end of 1997 there were 11 vessels (four conventional and seven ro-ro) operating. Ownership and chartering arrangements are relatively complex even for Poland for the vessels outlined in Figure 3.

In terms of the conventional vessels, one is owned by POL Levant and chartered to Levant Chartering of Malta (99% owned by POL Levant). It has a contract crew with Maltese flag and is chartered back to POL Levant on a time charter. Three conventional vessels are owned by Levant Shipping of Malta (99% owned by POL Levant), chartered to POL Levant on a time charter and Maltese flagged. Three other conventional vessels were owned by POL or POL America but have now been sold to Maltese interests owned by POL Levant and are bareboat chartered to POL Levant using POL Levant's

Figure 3
POL Levant Fleet - December 1996

VESSEL	DWT	TEU	YEAR BUILT	FLAG	TYPE
Bochnia	6372	46	1976	Malta	Con.
Chem	6388	46	1976	Malta	Con.
Garwolin	6380	46	1973	Malta	Con.
Ostrołęka	6380	46	1973	Poland	Con.
Radzionków	6380	46	1972	Malta	Con.
Siemiatycze	6380	46	1976	Malta	Con.
Wieliczka	6380	46	1973	Malta	Con.
Chodzież	8044	413	1988	Malta	Ro-ro
Tychy	8044	413	1988	Malta	Ro-ro
Włocławek	8044	413	1988	Malta	Ro-ro
Żerań	8044	413	1988	Poland	Ro-ro

Source: POL Levant, 1996

own Polish crew but under the Maltese flag.

In terms of ro-ro vessels, one is owned by POL/POL America, chartered in bare boat under Polish flag and the other three are owned by POL, time chartered from Levant Chartering of Malta and Maltese flagged.

All the convoluted chartering arrangements involving POL and POL America are arranged under commercial terms but, as quoted by a representative of POL Levant, have involved a considerable amount of good will on their part.

Two basic services are provided by the company - a Mediterranean ro-ro service with a sailing every 10 days and calling at either Gdynia, Aarhus, Valletta, Alexandria, Beirut, Lattakia and Limassol or Gdynia, Hamburg, Uddevalla, Alexandria, Beirut, Lattakia and Limassol. Tripoli (Libya), Tunis and Casablanca are served under inducement. A conventional service also operates every 10 days calling at Gdynia, Casablanca, Tunis, Tripoli (Libya), Istanbul, Benghazi, Tripoli (Lebanon), Alexandria, Lattakia, Beirut, Dordrecht and Antwerp. Representatives are retained in both Syria (in Lattakia) and Egypt (in Alexandria).

Cargo volume shipped during 1995 (as the last year for which reports are available) reached around 680000 tonnes of both general and bulk cargo which included around 150000 tonnes of containerised cargo representing 23% of the total. Four main areas of cargo activity in terms of southbound movements could be identified;

1) Polish cargo and transit from neighbouring countries via Polish ports, the latter dominated by trade from the Czech Republic, Lithuania, Slovakia and the CIS in descending order of importance.
2) Scandinavian cargo - in particular, Denmark, Sweden and Finland.
3) German cargo.
4) Benelux cargo.

The main products carried were processed steel sheets, wire and fabrications, paper on reels, industrial and commercial glass, tractors, milk powder, light bulbs, sugar and chemical products. Most products were provided through a variety of feeder lines in the Baltic from Finland (Kotka and Helsinki) or from direct inland access. A major problem for the company over the last two years has been the growth of competitors on the Baltic-Mediterranean route including Grimaldi Lines and Svenska Orient Line.

In a northbound direction traditional cargoes include potatoes, citrus fruit, cotton liners and sugar beet but supplemented more recently by steel products particularly from the Black Sea region. A number of additional services were also provided from and to Israel and Spain.

The structure of POL Levant is shown in Figure 4. The current (late 1997) owners of the company remain 49% POL, 49% EuroAfrica and 2% Polcontainer. This represents another manifestation of the complex commercialisation process that is going on in Poland at the moment and reflects the complexity of the ship ownership and flagging issue. Polcontainer is effectively 100% state owned whilst EuroAfrica remains at least in part owned by other state companies. Since POL is state owned this means that in practice, POL Levant is a majority state owned organisation, but because of the Polish laws on company ownership and its structure in terms of shareholdings, POL Levant is viewed legally as in the private sector thus benefiting from the lower tax regime and freedom of action that this brings.

The company has a number of its own equity investments which help to further complicate the commercialisation and ownership regimes. These include Eurolevant Shipping Limited of Malta, 99% of which is owned by POL Levant and operates POL Levant vessels under the Maltese flag; Levant Shipping Limited of Malta (99% owned) who own the tonnage chartered by POL Levant; Levant Chartering Limited of Malta (99% owned) who charter tonnage for POL Levant; POL-MARINE Limited of Gdynia (22% owned), insurance brokers; OY FIN-POL Shipping Limited of Helsinki (40% owned) who are the general agent for POL Levant in Finland and Morskie Biuro Prawne of Gdynia (11% owned) who are maritime lawyers. This pattern of joint ownership between POL companies is replicated throughout the subsidiaries.

Figure 4
POL Levant Company structure

SHAREHOLDERS

SUPERVISORY BOARD

BOARD OF DIRECTORS

MANAGING DIRECTOR

Economic Division	Secretarial Division
Shipping Department	Financial/Accounting Department
Deputy Managing Director Shipping Affairs	Deputy Managing Director Financial Affairs

Technical Division	Operating Division	Sales & Marketing Division	Financial Dept.	Accounting Dept.
Technical Supervision	Vessel Operations	Ro-ro	Cash	Accountant
		Conventional	Invoicing	Domestic Settlement
	Stevedoring	Tariffs &	Files	
	Settlement & Admin.	Statistics	Freight Recovery	Foreign Settlement
	Container Logistics			Cost Return
	Claims			

Source : POL Levant Annual Report 1996

The immediate effect of the move away from the parent company was dramatic. The traditional costing structures within POL, which did not relate costs to expenditures necessarily, were abandoned and accurate profit/loss centres were introduced - everything from container rental costs to bunkering and repairs. The existing system had been derived almost entirely from the politically driven economics dominant previous to the recent changes in Poland.

The result was a net profit for POL Levant from year one of its existence -

> 1993 - 580,400   new złoty (210,000US$)
> 1994 - 1,855,700 (650,000US$)
> 1995 - 3,657,800 (1,300,000US$)
> 1996 - 2,002,400 (700,000US$)

This represents a substantial growth in net profits (for example some 197.1% from 1994 to 1995) followed by a noticeable decline in 1996 which in the context of the troubled Polish shipping sector remains remarkable. Ranked on income level by a Gdańsk based newspaper, POL Levant emerged as the 21st highest company in the region, a ranking that would have been considerably higher amongst shipping companies if based on net profit. Other interesting financial statistics for 1995 show income tax payments of some 1,566,700 new złotys rising from 1,092,600 in 1994 and 485,300 the year before. This alone reflects real profit growth but also an increasing tax burden. The very large majority of all these profits was obtained from the company's basic activity of ship operations with only some 7.6% of profits emerging from ancillary activities. This has been an increasing proportion of the company's activities but reduced in 1996.

Data on POL Levant's shipping operations and cargo volumes are given in Figure 5.

Figure 5
POL Levant shipping operations and cargo volumes 1996

Origin	tonnes x 1000		%	%
	1995	1996	1995	1996
Polish foreign trade	180.0	183.8	26.4	28.6
Transit	59.6	56.8	8.7	8.8
Cross trade	442.5	401.6	64.9	62.6
TOTAL	682.1	642.2	100.0	100.0

Figure 5 continued

Type of cargo	tonnes x 1000		%	%
	1995	1996	1995	1996
General non refrig	468.7	429.7	68.7	66.9
Refrigerated	0.7	0	0.1	0
Containerised	153.2	159.1	22.5	24.8
Bulk	59.5	53.4	8.7	8.3
TOTAL	682	642	100.0	100.0

Source : POL Levant 1996

POL Levant presents some interesting issues in all this discussion of changes in the Polish shipping industry. We can note a number of them here before going on to look briefly at some of the other issues that stem from POL and its other subsidiary companies.

Firstly, there is the recurrent problem of reinvestment in ships. Despite the relatively high profitability of POL Levant particularly in comparison with many other shipping activities in Poland, there is not enough available money to finance the replacement of ships in the company and in particular for the African conventional service. The company recognises this problem and is looking towards the acquisition of second hand vessels to upgrade the infrastructure. This was likely to occur in late 1997.

Secondly, there is the continuing troubled relationship with the parent company POL - a relationship which in many ways remains like a double edged sword. On the one hand it is beneficial to be associated with the traditions and the marketing advantages of POL; but on the other it also reflects poorly on POL Levant to be associated with a debt laden ancestor from the old regime. The relationship at times also remains unclear to all parties, particularly in the tax and finance areas and the responsibility of each organisation.

Thirdly, the results achieved so far by the company are commendable but, by their own admission, much remains to be done. In particular, the company aims to purchase three conventional and one ro-ro vessel from POL thus consolidating operations and ownership into the company. Short term ambitions also include achievement of ISO9002 and the ISM Code certificates.

Finally, POL Levant is a successful company and one that looks ripe for full privatisation as soon as is possible. It is noteworthy that the separation of the company from POL appears to have produced the results that would have been hoped for and it is little wonder that further separations have been pursued since then.

Other subsidiaries

We will now turn our attention to the other subsidiary companies which have been spun off from POL to provide a brief review of the new organisational structure (11). Each of these subsidiaries has been established to achieve a level of autonomy in their operations and to provide an independent incentive to develop services, improve quality and to make more precise the flow of costs and income that results. Other reasons for their introduction include a need to divest POL of activities so that they are protected from the unsatisfactory debt conditions that exist in the parent company, and finally to prepare the way towards privatisation which is only feasible through the divestment of small and identifiable operating units. Each will be described briefly in turn whilst details of ship services are contained in Figure 6:-

(1) *EuroAfrica Linie* - emerged as the first part of the reformed POL in the process of restructuring the state owned parent, when it was separated off on 1st September 1991 and released to operate independently. Before then it had been the Szczecin branch of the liner shipping activities of POL with specialisms in services to Finland, the UK, Eire and West Africa. The initial major investor was POL, but subsequently private individual investors, the Gdynia Port Authority, Szczecin-Świnoujście Port Authority and a number of other private companies have become part owners. EuroAfrica was the first privately owned element of the Polish maritime sector (see later chapter for more details).

(2) *Franck and Tobiesen Poland Sp. z.o.o.* - based in Gdynia, was separated from POL on 1st January 1993. The company provides trucking services with around 100 western built Volvo tractors and 110 trailers to countries across central and Eastern Europe. It also provides clearance and port agency services for vessels to Gdynia and customs clearance, forwarding and brokerage services.

(3) *Polcontainer Sp. z.o.o.* - is based in Gdynia, and was the second POL subsidiary to be produced from the original POL parent company on 1st July 1992. On 1st May 1996, the company was restructured as a totally

19

independent company. It operates under an agency contract to POL providing container logistics, roll and mafi trailers for the shipping lines and organises, manages and controls container traffic in Poland and beyond. Services are also provided independently for EuroAfrica in Szczecin, POL Levant, POL America and POL SEAL in Gdynia and a variety of overseas organisations in Poland.

(4) *POL-America Inc.* - is the largest of the POL subsidiaries and was the fourth company established on 1st June 1993 operating shipping services to South American ports - both west and east coasts and to Central America, the Caribbean and the US Gulf. It emerged from an earlier form as Polskie Towarzystwo Okęrtowe S.A., a joint stock company which was owned by Warta Insurance and Bank Polska Kasa Opiecki S.A.. Although it has offices in Gdynia it is formally incorporated in the United States. The company operates four semi-container vessels on the west coast line (including reefer space, container storage, tanks for liquid cargo and passenger accommodation for up to 12 voyagers), two vessels on the central American, Caribbean and US Gulf line (including tanks for liquids, reefer container slots and passenger accommodation) and four more vessels on the east coast line (including reefer container slots, heavy lifts, general cargo space and passenger accommodation). Recent developments in services have included new connections to and from Bilbao (Spain), Kaliningrad (Russia) and Tallin (Estonia). Its ownership of vessels fluctuates regularly over time and frequently the company operates vessels owned by POL. In January 1996, POL America was the first POL subsidiary to operate a new building in the POL group for many years with the acquisition of the 16000 DWT "Luta" from the Galatz (Romania) shipyard. Between 20 and 28 ships representing a total of 270-300000 DWT were operated in 1996 although another 13 amounting to 179267 DWT also passed through the company's responsibilities. Sailings are programmed for every three weeks to both east and west coasts of South America.

Employment at POL America amounts to around 50 shore based staff and 665 vessel crew at the end of 1996. The company itself was divided up into seven divisions - vessels, marketing, shipping, technical, financial, marine and administration with the whole organisation led by a chief executive and a separate chairman.

In a similar fashion to most POL group companies, POL America has substantial shareholdings in a variety of subsidiary companies These include Franck and Tobiesen Poland (100% owned, Gdynia based truckers and forwarders), Baltic Container Lines (40%, Gdynia based ship operators providing feeder services to and from Gdynia, Bremerhaven and Hamburg and set up in collaboration with the Port of Gdynia.), Emerald Shipping

(99%, Cyprus based ship owners), Polocean - W. Sikorski Shipping (99%, Cyprus based ship owners), Polocean - S. Starzynski Shipping (99%, Cyprus based ship owners), POL Marine (22%, Gdynia based insurance and claims brokers) and Maritime Law Office Co. (11%, Gdynia based legal consultants).

(5) *POL-SEAL Shipping Lines Sp. z.o.o.* - also based in Gdynia, was incorporated on the 1st June 1994, employing four vessels between European and East and South African ports, including Gdynia, Antwerp, Aqaba, Port Sudan, Mombasa, Dar-es-Salaam and Durban. Frequency of service is low at one trip every eight weeks and is based upon four semi-container vessels incorporating reefer facilities, tanks and passenger accommodation.

(6) *POL Asia and POL Atlantic* are two relatively new companies, both based in Gdynia, spun off on the 1st March 1996 acting as the operators on the Far East/Australian and North American (Canada, USA, Gulf of Mexico) markets. The former is co-operating closely with Singapore based Neptune Orient Line. Both are independent from POL but neither have tonnage of their own buying in slots in this market and replacing the previously existing POL Fesa and POL Eureca which had been earlier subsidiaries to the parent. POL Atlantic charters slots from other North Atantic operators - more specifically ACL (800 TEU weekly to the US East Coast and Canada) and MSC (450 TEU every 10 days to the Gulf of Mexico) although prior to 1993 they operated their own vessels on the route. Severe financial losses forced them to change their approach to the market with the immediate effect of turning the losses into a small profit which has been sustained and improved upon ever since. For example, the immediate effect upon loadings was to reduce TEUs from 148000 to 135000 from 1992 (utilising their own ships) to 1993 (using others) and the obvious reduction in costs that this slot chartering approach brought. POL Atlantic was a founder member of the Trans Atlantic Agreement which has attempted, through its successor TACA, to maintain and sustain prices on the sector but which continues to face legal problems from both the European Union and the Federal Maritime Commission (USA) over anti-competitive practices.

Recent moves by POL have suggested that as a consequence of high loadings, they may enter the North Atlantic market themselves in the near future with two 3000 TEU vessels whilst retaining their slot charters with MSC and ACL (1). However, delays in implementing this policy are occurring due to a dispute over the slot charter agreement with MSC that the latter claims precludes POL Atlantic from taking this step.

(7) *POL Supply Sp. z.o.o.* provides a complete supply service to vessels including everything from mechanical equipment to catering, transport facilities for goods and persons to and from vessels and ports both within Poland and abroad, forwarding services, import-export services and storage in owned warehouses of 11000sqm. *POL Catering Sp. z.o.o.* provide specialist catering services for the maritime sector; *POL Crewing Sp. z.o.o.* provide an increasingly large crew agency service for any vessels - including those of POL and its subsidiaries (25,28). The company emerged from the personnel department of Polish Ocean Lines and now places around 3000 crew members a year, of which around 1800 are with international owners. Pay-roll, insurance and training services are also provided for other POL subsidiary companies. Employment at POL Crewing has declined from a peak of about 80 and continues to decline to around 25 - 30. All three companies are based in Gdynia.

Meanwhile *Euro East Lines* of Luxembourg is a joint POL and Belgian company operating seven general cargo vessels purchased from POL on routes from the Baltic and the Mediterranean to Thailand and Indonesia. Separate companies provide agency services in Poland - *Euro East Maritime Agency Sp. z.o.o.* (Gdynia) and *Euro East Agency N.V.* (Antwerp). The ships are flagged in Luxembourg but still crewed by POL.

Table 6 : POL shipping services

Company	Frequency	Ports
Far East		
POL Asia (slot charter with NOL)	2 weekly FCL only	Hamburg, Bremerhaven, Colombo, Port Kelang, Singapore, Pusan, Kaoshiung Hong Kong
Australia		
POL Asia (slot charter with MSC)	weekly FCL only	Gdynia, Bremerhaven, Freemantle, Adelaide, Sydney, Brisbane, Melbourne
Middle East		
POL Asia (slot charter with CMB)	every 6 days	Felixstowe, Hamburg, Antwerp, Jebel Ali, Karachi, Nhava Sheva

Table 6 continued

US Gulf

POL Atlantic (slot charter with MSC)	weekly FCL only	Antwerp, Bremerhaven, Gdynia, Felixstowe, Wilmington, Charleston, Miami, New Orleans, Houston

North Atlantic

POL Atlantic (slot charter with ACL & MSC)	weekly	Le Havre, Hamburg, Felixstowe, Halifax, Boston, Gothenburg, Liverpool
POL Atlantic (slot charter with ACL & MSC)	2 weekly	Gdynia, Antwerp, Bremerhaven, New York, Baltimore, Portsmouth

United Kingdom

EuroAfrica (with United Baltic)	2 weekly	Gdynia, Felixstowe, Hull

West Africa

EuroAfrica	2 monthly	Szczecin, Uddevalla, Antwerp, Banjul, Abidjan, Tema, Lagos, Doula

Sweden

EuroAfrica	3 daily Pass/rail/car ferry	Świnoujście, Ystad

Eire

EuroAfrica	2 monthly	Szczecin, Dublin

Finland

EuroAfrica	weekly	Szczecin, Turku, Helsinki, Gdynia
EuroAfrica	weekly	Gdynia, Helsinki, Kotka

Table 6 continued

Mediterranean

POL Levant	2 monthly ro-ro	Gdynia, Aarhus, Uddevalla, Hamburg, Casablanca, Tunis, Valletta, Beirut, Alexandria, Lattakia, Limassol
POL Levant	2 monthly conventional	Gdynia, Antwerp, Casablanca, Tunis, Tripoli, Benghazi, Alexandria, Lattakia, Beirut, Haifa, Ashdod

East and South
Africa

POL Seal	every 8 weeks	Gdynia, Antwerp/Marseilles, Aqaba, Jeddah, Port Sudan, Eritrea, Comoro Is, Mombasa, Dar es Salaam, Durban, West Coast Africa, Gdynia

Central America
Caribbean
US Gulf

POL America	monthly	Gdynia, Uddevalla, Santa Domingo, La Guaira/Port Cabello, Cartegena, Pto. Limon/Sto. Tomas de Castella, Kingston, Lake Charles, Tampico, Orinoco, Rotterdam, Hamburg, Tallinn

South America
East Coast

POL America	every 3 weeks	Tallinn, Kaliningrad, Gdynia, Uddevalla, Bilbao, Santos, Montevideo, Buenos Aires, Salvador, Casablanca, Leixoes, Rotterdam

Table 6 continued

South America
West Coast
POL America   every 3 weeks   Gdynia, Uddevalla, Hamburg,
                                               Antwerp, Bilbao, Guayaquil,
                                               Callao, Valparaiso, Pisco,
                                               Rotterdam, Hamburg/Bremen,
                                               Kaliningrad, Klaipeda/Ventspils

Feeder service
POL Atlantic   twice weekly   Gdynia and Bremerhaven

Source : POL, 1997

This rather complex set of companies which has emerged from the original conglomerate of POL has been distanced, at least to a certain extent, from the parent company. POL itself still exists, based in Gdynia, and with a very close working (and personal) relationship with all its subsidiaries. Much of the work done by each is on behalf of other subsidiaries or POL. POL now still owns most of the property of the group as a whole, leasing it to the subsidiaries where this seems appropriate. However, POL does not operate any ships nor any other type of practical operational work. In theory, the subsidiary companies carry out all these activities on behalf of POL on a clear financial basis leaving the subsidiaries to work for others when they wish and to survive or die according to their economic success. Subsidiaries must plan their own operations, investment and finances and are left independent to so do - as shown by the activities of POL Levant. This does not mean that POL and the other subsidiaries are not dominant clients in many circumstances, but it should mean no cross subsidies and financial strengthening through ownership of responsibility in smaller operating units.

Consolidating the structure within the group and in particular the relationships between its elements is the first stage in the creation of State Treasury Exclusive Company (STEC) status for POL - this would be the first real stage towards privatisation but is unlikely to make much progress before 1999 when the new structure will have settled down. By then the continuing problem of POL debt, which has troubled the company for many years and which peaked in 1993 when a liquidity crisis forced the Treasury to impose a managing director directly under their control, should have improved somewhat, with clearer financial control and successive changes in Polish business law. In 1995 alone, POL's debt was reduced to one third of 1994 and although that sort of speed of reduction cannot continue, plans for POL to become a joint stock company and reduce debt further through a debt for equity plan, already exist (31).

Discussion

The situation that surrounds the development, in fact the survival of the POL empire is one that in many ways typifies that of the Polish shipping industry as it transforms from the dinosaur companies of the state sector pre-changes to the new and dynamic marketplace of the late twentieth century. Somehow POL as an organisation is still in existence, albeit much reduced in size and power and no longer an operator of anything in its own right although still a major shipowner. In some ways the worst of the transformation stage has probably passed - profits of US$7m were posted in 1996 for the first time in seven years and contrasted with a loss of US$12m the year before. This in turn has encouraged POL to invest in ships for the first time in many years when they purchased four second-hand vessels from the Polish-Chinese operator Chipolbrok and a single new-building in the "Luta" for POL America. The four second hand vessels are intended for subsidiary services to the Far East, South America and West Africa. Further vessel acquisition is expected to result in the reintroduction in the foreseeable future of POL group vessels on the north Atlantic during 1998. Four vessels were scrapped in 1996/7 and three new buildings are planned for 1998. Incidentally, finance for all new acquisitions is anticipated to come from foreign sources to the tune of 90% (between US$ 250 and 270m) as Polish banks remain largely unwilling (or unable) to provide resources to the industry.

Today POL provides support and marketing power as a group leader channelling business into a series of small operating companies that have taken on the role previously that of the parent in the market place and diversified their clients to increase independence and financial strength. This does, however, beg one or two questions. What is the true relationship between POL and its subsidiaries and are the financial and supportive agreements conducted on a purely commercial basis? What are the real prospects for privatisation in both the parent group and the subsidiaries? At the moment the prospects in the latter do appear to be much greater than the former as they are associated with distinct markets, have a clear idea of what operating in the commercial sector means and, in some cases (e.g. POL Levant and POL America) make reasonable profits. POL itself is a different beast altogether. It remains state owned and as such still displays the characteristics of an organisation that is reluctant to be exposed to market forces - and realistically, if it was, soon would fade and die. It remains in existence for a combination of political reasons - it is unacceptable to lose a major state company - and because of strenuous financial and organisational efforts by the state to retain it. It would seem a realistic scenario for the not too distant future however, that POL is allowed to reduce its activities as the newly privatised subsidiaries spread their market influence and inevitably become more independent. In another chapter dealing with EuroAfrica - one of the privatised subsidiaries, now minority owned by POL - their comments on ownership centre on their desire to avoid control by their old parent and to move further from the practices and organisational structures of the past. This is perhaps indicative of what may develop in the future. In contrast to this, POL announced that they had purchased a new vessel in February (the 16100 DWT "Luta", built in Romania) for the first time in many years and consideration was being given to the purchase of a second, possibly indicating at least some change in fortune.

Meanwhile, the subsidiaries continue to take from POL what they can, in terms of marketing in particular, and an uneasy relationship exists between each of the two groups. It will be particularly interesting to see how this relationship develops.

In terms of commercialisation throughout all of the companies discussed here there is a clear divide between the subsidiaries, and particularly those with the longest history - i.e. EuroAfrica, POL Levant, POL America and Polcontainer - and POL itself. Those firmly located in the market place now show most of the characteristics of private shipping firms including everything from financial practice, foreign flagging, and employment regimes to those of office equipment and most importantly of all, attitude to clients and potential markets. This difference will develop further, possibly isolating POL itself from its own subsidiary companies. If POL is to survive it must adapt to these new conditions and in particular, establish a role for itself in the new shipping market developing in Poland and find a realistic way to privatise its own activites. The most likely approach to the latter is to convert into equity the substantial debt it still faces so that creditors of the company would become owners of a stake in the operation It also plans to diversify and in late 1997 was entering the tourism market through hotel development and looking to extend this activity with a joint venture in the Gdynia region. There are some early signs that the privatisation and liberalisation process is now really happening, with some 14 of its 15 subsidiaries now making some form of profit but there remains a long way to go yet before the whole organisation can be confident of its future.

In the meantime Polish Ocean Lines remains one of the most interesting and contentious of all the industrial sectors of the maritime economy of Poland and in many ways of Eastern Europe as a whole. It represents both the best and the worst of what can be seen across the sector at the moment reflecting the dynamism of the shipping industry as it attempts to adapt and change to the new pressures being placed upon it and the constraints that continue to remain from the old system from which it has emerged.

Polsteam Tankers Limited

The company

Polsteam Tankers Limited is a specialist tanker operating company based in Gdynia with associated harbour offices in Gdynia and Gdańsk ports. The company was formed in 1993 from the tanker side of PZM, the state owned bulk carrier operator based in Szczecin but had always operated as a separate branch from its offices in Gdynia. It is one of three spin-off ship operating companies formed from the parent group the others being Polsteam Shortramp and Polsteam Oceantramp. Polsteam Tankers is by far the smallest of the three. Originally, in 1993, it had continued to provide services in its established markets of crude oil and liquid (or molten) sulphur. However, with the ever increasing pressure on the company to survive in a liberalised market place, the difficulties of the crude oil market had encouraged the company to concentrate on a niche product - i.e. liquid sulphur. In very recent months, however, the upturn in the crude market had suggested that they should once again look in that direction for diversification although by late 1997, no tangible moves had been made. A series of other products were also being examined to increase diversification, but the company refused to be specific about these.

The company has a rather complex relationship with its originator and mother company PZM. Partial privatisation has actually taken place with some 30% of the company shares owned by employees of Polsteam. The remaining 70% is owned either directly by PZM, or by a series of other companies owned by PZM. As the parent company remains state owned at the moment, and consequently large chunks (if not all) of the other owning companies are state owned, then Polsteam, to all intents and purposes is a state owned company as well with a small element of private investment. However, under Polish company law, since Polsteam and PZM are constituted as Joint Stock Companies and not directly managed and owned as state departments (unlike for example the railways - PKP, PZM or Polish Ocean Lines) they are treated as private companies and thus benefit from various tax exemptions (e.g. company tax is constrained to 40% - 38% from 1997) and freedoms of expenditure and state control. No longer is the Ministry of Transport or the Treasury a major influence on company strategy and the vast majority of decisions are local at least to PZM and its associated companies and most commonly to Polsteam itself.

Polsteam owns no vessels at all but manages the entire fleet of five tankers which remain owned by PZM. Two of these tankers are effectively laid up in Gdynia in late 1997, with plans to scrap one of them soon. The other is destined to be reactivated for the liquid sulphur or crude oil market in the near future.

Clearly, the liquid sulphur market is very important to the company and represents a deliberate attempt to specialise in a niche market area where Polsteam has proven expertise and can be almost sure of making a reasonable profit. This represents, as a result, a major step forward in terms of approach to the market compared with the old regime in the bulk market place where a market presence, even in trades where little or no money could be made, was a tactical requirement for Polish state owned shipping companies.

The liquid sulphur trade is very small but significant in that it is a vital commodity in the production of fertilisers. In late 1996 there were only 11 specially equipped tankers world-wide under the control of US, Mexican and Japanese firms in addition to Polsteam. PZM originally got involved in the trade in 1973 with the 9800 DWT Tarnobrzeg (now Tarnobrzeg II) which is one of the vessels laid up in Gdynia and also the one likely to be scrapped soon. Liftings of sulphur by Polsteam in 1995 were up from 440000 tonnes the previous year to 512000 tonnes. Profits were reported as high, for the first time since 1989.

The market has changed characteristics considerably since the early 1970s, shifting from carrying the raw material in liquefied form from source countries - including Poland - to transporting it from refineries where it is produced in ever increasing quantities artificially - partly as a result of dwindling natural sources and increasingly as a result of severe environmental pressures. Polsteam has tended to concentrate upon limited geographical markets as well specialising on trades between Poland, North Africa, Western Europe and Scandinavia; and Japan and Indonesia.

Polsteam's fleet in late 1997 consisted of the following vessels;

Penelope - Liquid sulphur and sulphuric acid carrier with a DWT of 15329. Delivered in 1996, this 8565 cu. m. capacity vessel was originally destined to be a bulk carrier. The hull was built at the Stocznia Szczecinska yard in Szczecin and transferred for tank installation and completion to Gdańska Stocznia Remontowa, the shiprepair yard in Gdańsk. Bahamas registered, she conducted her maiden voyage in April 1996 between Germany and North Carolina (USA) but has now been allocated to an eight year charter for the trade between Japan and Indonesia. As with all modern liquid sulphur carriers, the *Penelope* is fitted with heating coils in her cargo section to keep the cargo molten at around 135-140 degC. The owner of the vessel is Ina Shipping Ltd of Monrovia (Liberia), a condition of the financiers, and allowing Polsteam to flag the vessel with the Bahamas.

Zaglebie Siarkowe - Liquid sulphur carrier of 11309 cu. m. capacity and a DWT of 9783. Built in 1976 and still active in the market place. The owner of the vessel is ZPSA - Żegluga Polska SA of Szczecin, a wholly owned subsidiary of PZM. Polish flagged.

Prof K. Bohdanowicz - Product carrier built in 1974 and still active in the market place. 9694 DWT and a capacity of 11310 cub.m.. Owner is ZPSA of Szczecin. Polish flagged.

Siarkopol - Product carrier built in 1974 but now laid up in Gdynia possibly awaiting conversion. Capacity of 11656 cub. m. and a DWT of 9750. Owned by ZPSA of Szczecin. Polish flagged.

Tarnobrzeg II - Liquid sulphur carrier built in 1974 of 9814 DWT. Capacity 11648 cub. m. and owned by ZPSA of Szczecin. Laid up awaiting probable scrapping.

All the above vessels, apart from the *Penelope*, are registered under the Polish flag and manned with Polish crew and officers. The *Penelope* was registered in the Bahamas as a requirement of the banks that provided the finance for her purchase. She is owned by Ina Shipping of Liberia also for financial reasons. Polsteam has a management agreement with its parent company PZM, to provide shipping services whereby Polsteam provide the organisational and marketing input and PZM provide the ships, crews, officers except for on the new vessel where PZM crews are not used.

Two more liquid sulphur vessels are on order from the Szczecin shipbuilder's yard, of 15300 DWT each. They are due for delivery in 1998 and 1999. Both will have a cubic capacity of 8500m and are similar in design to the *Penelope*. These latter two vessels are destined to replace *Tarnobrzeg II and Prof K. Bohdanowicz* in the European markets and have been financed through a $42m term loan over 8 years arranged by MeesPierson which also covered the purchase of the *Penelope*.

Polsteam itself is divided into three operational divisions with 38 staff members in its headquarters in Gdynia and an agency office in Gdańsk. The three divisions are:

- Ship operations.
- Ship management.
- Agency services.

The ship operation division has grown out of more than 20 years of tanker operations which originated through the PZM activities of the early 1970s in the markets of Suezmax, product carriers and liquid sulphur carriers. As noted earlier, the company has now focused down onto the last of these three as a specialised and potentially profitable activity. This division has the responsibility of organising chartering, operations, agency, crewing management, dry-docking, surveys, insurance, P and I activities and the purchase and delivery of stores and spares.

The ship management division provides a complete ship management service which commonly borrows expertise and resources from the parent company of PZM. Quality assurance is guaranteed as the division has already obtained ISO 9002. Economic competitiveness is ensured through the widespread use of Polish crews taken from PZM's pool of labour and other locally available facilities.

Agency services are provided at the ports of Gdynia and Gdańsk including the services of full ship agency, crew attendance, bunkering and catering. Although specialising in tankers, all types of vessel can be accommodated.

In terms of day to day operational structure, the company is actually divided into technical, operations, agency and finance and administration sections which overly the structure presented in the market place. Thus, for example, the finance and technical activities of Polsteam would feature in the operations, management and agency divisions.

Polsteam Tankers is represented abroad in a large number of countries either through subsidiary organisations of the PZM group - for example in Luxembourg, Netherlands, USA, UK, Spain and Brazil - or by direct representatives in Italy, Sweden, Tunisia, Germany, Morocco and France.

Discussion

A number of significant issues arise from this discussion of Polsteam Tankers which in the light of recent political, social and economic change, need discussion, interpretation and illumination.

First and foremost there is the rather confused relationship between the parent company (PZM) and Polsteam Tankers (and for that matter the other spin-off companies of Polsteam Oceantramp and Polsteam Shortramp). In terms of Polish business law Polsteam Tankers is a private company with all the privileges that that brings in terms of tax payments, workers councils and the exemption from the requirements to consult and gain acceptance of decisions and in terms of company constitution and responsibilities. However, it remains the case that Polsteam Tankers is still tightly entrenched within the sphere of PZM and in particular, has very close financial relationships in terms of profit, movement of cash and potentially cross-subsidy. This is especially relevant for two reasons - the first is that it means that the independent Polsteam Tankers is in many ways a falsehood and that unlike many western companies, the development of subsidiary and independent organisations has not in reality, been achieved. Polsteam Tankers acts in effect like a distanced department of the parent. Secondly, it needs to be remembered that PZM remains wholly state owned and although restructured, remains under the indirect and influential guidance of the Polish government. Consequently, much of what Polsteam Tankers does is effectively under the umbrella of a state organisation - albeit one in a rather different financial and economic climate compared with ten years ago.

Secondly, there remains some evidence of indirect subsidy into the sector generally, of which Polsteam Tankers gains its share - for example the application of zero value added tax for the shipping industry. More specifically, there remains a major question mark over the indirect subsidy provided by PZM through uncommercial arrangements for property letting to Polsteam Tankers who continue to receive subsidised, if not free accommodation in Gdynia. Admittedly the structures for commercial property letting (and other service provision) now exist generally and any state or private company would have to pay a commercial rate in the free market, but there remain extensive anomalies within company groups that do not mirror the true cost centred approach of the west.

Thirdly, Polsteam Tankers represents a typical adaptation of the true Joint Stock Company principle - and that of privatisation - that has become common in Poland and under Polish company law. The main owner of Polsteam Tankers remains the state, even if this is through a rather convoluted process dominated by PZM in Szczecin and their associated companies. Certainly some rather diluted form of privatisation exists through the minority employee ownership, but inevitably the state influence continues to persist. This is by no means the same as the old relationship between enterprise and state ministry whereby all decisions of any size would have had to pass through Warsaw as well as the large majority of resources. Polsteam Tankers has considerable independence from PZM, and PZM itself now has some independence from the state and hence the effect is notably indirect. However, the attitude, and philosophy remains some way from that of true privatisation and it is highly debatable whether a financially failing Polsteam Tankers would be allowed to go bankrupt even though the technical possibility is now there. Certainly the current situation represents some progress towards a full exposure of the company to the private market place but with some way to go. PZM's influence remains strong through the detailed linkages that exist - e.g. including their dictation of crews, ships, markets, finance and corporate image.

Despite these rather harsh conclusions it is only fair to emphasise the progress towards full privatisation that has been made and the amount of adaptation to a market led position. Considerable adaptation to market demands are clearly evident - including the upgrading of vessels and entry into new market locations around the world - plus obvious changes in personnel structure, office design and image and some appreciation of the role of marketing. Given the starting point as a department within PZM in the early 1990s within a state controlled industry, Polsteam Tankers' adaptation so far has been creditable if far from complete. Their prospects are reasonably good given a dominant position within a niche market coupled with the inheritance of a number of advantages from the old system.

EuroAfrica Linie Żeglugowe Sp. z.o.o.

Introduction

EuroAfrica Linie emerged as the first part of the reformed Polish Ocean Lines in the process of restructuring the state owned liner shipping company, when it was separated off from the mother organisation in 1990 and released to operate independently within the newly liberalised market place that was created from that year in Polish shipping. Up until that time, it had been the commercial shipping department of the Polish Ocean Lines empire, located in Szczecin, unlike the vast majority of the company that had its location in Gdynia - where most of the other offshoots and the parent company still are. EuroAfrica was thus initially state owned like all the new subsidiaries and it is only in recent years that it has moved more towards the private sector - something that we shall return to in the next section. In 1991, the company became a limited liability company with the majority of shares owned by Polish Ocean Lines. This represented the first stage in reforming the ownership structure.

EuroAfrica undertook responsibility for the old Szczecin based POL liner services particularly focusing upon the UK and Ireland service and those to West Africa utilising a variety of container and conventional facilities. To this day, this remains their main area of concern although considerable expansion has occurred into the ferry business and to other European destinations for container services (9).

Ownership

As we have seen already, EuroAfrica was at the forefront of the process of ownership change that has occurred so far in the Polish maritime sector representing the first of the parts of the state owned shipping enterprises to be given any semblance of independence and subsequently, limited liability status with the opportunity to vary the shareholder profiles that existed, Although the initial main owner was POL, who by 1992 possessed some 48.70% of the shares, this was substantially less than the effective 100% that was owned prior to 1990. In 1992, some 11.50% of shares were taken up by private persons (largely company employees), 1.00% by the Szczecin-Świnoujście Port Authority and 38.80% by other, private companies. However, it is important to note at this stage and for future discussion, that the vast majority of these "private" companies are, in fact reconstituted state companies that are nominally in the private sector under Polish business law, but in many cases are entirely, or at least largely, still owned by the state albeit subject to the company laws relating to accounts, bankruptcies etc. By early 1997 ownership structure was some 27.68% still owned by POL, 57.25% by private companies (still largely state derived "private" sector concerns), 7.14% by the Port Authority of Gdynia, 0.71% by the Szczecin-Świnoujście Port Authority and 7.22% by private persons. However, in late 1997, further ownership changes took place as we shall detail later. Figures 7 and 8 give the details of the trends in ownership and how they have changed over the period between 1992 and the end of 1995 and reaffirms the continued lack of true private capital or involvement from the private sector and the complete absence of overseas investment. Examples of the private company owners that exist include Polcontainer - a POL company - with some 9% of shares, that remains largely state owned; Polska Żegluga Morska (PZM), the state owned bulk carrier company; and Pekaes Speditor, the formerly state owned international trucking company. We shall see as we go on how the exchange and cross ownership of shares in these "private" companies is highly convoluted and heavily entwined. Two things in particular need to be noted from these figures. Firstly, the apparent decline in the share of that POL holds in the ownership of EuroAfrica from a peak of 48.70% in 1992, to a more recent lower level of 27.68%. This disguises the actual fact that much of the previous ownership has now moved with the divestment of small filial companies by POL and the ownership structure has, therefore not really changed much at all. Secondly, the decline in state ownership in EuroAfrica is also a function of the changes occurring between 1992 and the end of 1995, in that the new filial companies, as noted earlier, are legally defined as private (and thus the shares they own in EuroAfrica are also privately owned) and yet the majority of these companies are actually still owned themselves by state companies. Thus the move of EuroAfrica towards private ownership is rather less pronounced than appears to be the case.

Figure 7
Shareholders in EuroAfrica 1992-1995 (%)

	1992	1993	1994	1995
OWNER				
Polish Ocean Lines	48.70	38.74	27.68	27.68
Employees	11.50	11.46	8.51	7.22
Szczecin-Świnoujście P.A.	1.00	1.00	0.71	0.71
Gdynia P.A.	0	10.00	7.14	7.14
Private Companies	38.80	38.80	55.96	57.25

Source: EuroAfrica Annual Report 1995

EuroAfrica sees a large number of benefits in the variety and types of owners that they currently have and also in moves to ensure that certain trends in ownership are constrained as much as is possible. In terms of the POL element of ownership, benefits have been gained in the availability of cheap ships and in terms of preferential commercial treatment over a variety of issues. The practice of low cost chartering continues to this day. There remains a determination by POL, to return to the North American market, in terms of actual ship operation (POL abandoned ship operation in 1992 retaining only a slot charter agreement with three other operators), and this it is hoped will be achieved through close collaboration with EuroAfrica to the mutual benefit of both companies. One drawback of POL involvement, however, is the continued down market image of the original parent company that EuroAfrica would like to be rid of, and also the ever present fear that in a truly liberalised market POL could eventually buy their way back in to ownership of the company and thus return to haunt the relatively progressive EuroAfrica operation. PZM investment is felt to be generally beneficial as their financial base is very strong and their international reputation very good despite their continued state ownership.

Figure 8
Shareholders in EuroAfrica by Category of Ownership 1992-1995

		1992	1993	1994	1995
OWNER					
State	No.	12,425	12,436	12,436	12,436
Enterprises	%	49.70	49.74	35.53	35.53
Private	No.	9,700	9,700	19,586	20,036
Companies	%	38,80	38.80	55.96	57.25
Employees	No.	2,875	2,864	2,976	2,528
	%	11.50	11.46	8.51	7.22
TOTAL	No.	25,000	25,000	35,000	35,000
	%	100.00	100.00	100.00	100.00

Source: EuroAfrica Annual report 1995

The respective port interests are welcomed simply because of the company's extensive use of port facilities. We shall return to the issue of ownership and equity investments later in this chapter. Suffice to say at the moment that the issue remains complex, flexible and fluctuating well into the late 1990s and as such provides much to discuss and ponder. EuroAfrica intends to implement a full private company operation and philosophy but has recognised that this will take time to impose fully and thus in their own words "will need support until they can face the market". A persistent complaint from the senior management has been that the newly invading western competition - for example Maersk container operations - has penetrated the market, for example between Poland and West Africa through the use of what they called "dumping" prices, (claimed to be around 50% of EuroAfrica rates) and well under the commercial rates that operators like EuroAfrica need to charge to survive. EuroAfrica's attempts to become free of any state support or protection is not helped by such predatory competition, and yet at the same time, the process of liberalisation is made more necessary by the need to compete with western operators. This conundrum remains unresolved and is likely to do so for some time (Figure 7).

Company structure

EuroAfrica has adopted a company structure that mirrors that of many west European companies and contrasts notably with the organisation that exists in most state owned companies. At the Head of the company are the shareholders - as we saw earlier these constitute a variety of types of organisations (Figure 8) but predominantly private investors, at least as defined by Polish business law. These shareholders are supported by a Supervisory Board that acts as the mechanism to ensure good relations and information flow between the shareholder level and the Board of Directors below it. In early 1996 this Board of Directors constituted the Managing Director, Deputy Managing Director, Financial Director and Technical Director with reasonably obvious responsibilities within the company. The Managing Director reports directly to the Board and on from there and has beneath him through the other respective directors, divisions for operations, technical issues and finance. Finally, operations are divided into the respective lines - West Africa, Finland, United Kingdom and Eire (Figure 9).

EuroAfrica fleet

The operating fleet of the EuroAfrica company at the end of 1996 stood as is shown in Figure 10. The fleet is dominated by a series of conventional vessels which are utilised on the West Africa run outlined in the next section. In addition to this are a number of ro-ro vessels which are allocated to the UK and Finnish trades and semi container vessels used on the Ireland trade or chartered out to foreign operators. Finally there are two rail-car ferries operating between Poland and Sweden. A final vessel involvement, as we shall see later is a part share in the "Polonia" operated by Unity Line in conjunction with ZPSA, part of the PZM empire.

Ownership of these vessels varied between two owned by the company, five with foreign flags chartered in and another eight chartered in from Polish Ocean Lines. The respective tonnages of these categories are 12786, 32180 and 51066 DWT. All EuroAfrica operated vessels provide facilities for accommodating passengers to meet a demand and style that lingers on from the old regime even though the company itself did not exist then. These eight Polish flagged vessels will not remain this way for long as there are active plans to reflag seven of them to flags of convenience for purely financial reasons. The only exception is the "Inowrocław", allotted until late 1997 to the Poland-United Kingdom run (Gdynia/Felixstowe/Hull), when it was replaced by a conventional lo-lo container vessel and which under the terms of the agreement with Polish Ocean Lines from whom it was obtained when EuroAfrica was set up, the crewing and flag arrangements must remain in Polish hands.

Figure 9
Company Organisation - EuroAfrica

SHAREHOLDERS

SUPERVISORY BOARD

BOARD OF DIRECTORS

MANAGING DIRECTOR

Administration	Finance	Technical Director	Deputy MD Director
	Financial Division	Technical Division	Operating Division
			West Africa Line	Finland Line	Ireland Line	UK Line

Source: EuroAfrica, 1996

Flags currently used include Cyprus, the Bahamas and St Vincent and Grenadine. Reflagging of all vessels is seen as preferable by the company because of a combination of Polish pension fund requirements and payments and the costs of insurance in addition to the more conventionally quoted issues emerging from the prohibitive cost of domestic seafarers. This latter issue is made more untenable by the 48% taxation rate on seafarers' salaries in Poland. However, all these financial issues may be made easier by a planned relaxation of taxation requirements on replacement of vessels due to come into force in 1997.

The proposed second Polish register, which in the traditional style of such registers (e.g. NIS, DIS, Isle of Man) will attempt to provide relatively high registration standards whilst relaxing the expensive crewing rules of the main Polish register, should help to bring some relief to the beleaguered shipping industry and possibly stem the flow of vessels to flags of convenience. This will also offer an alternative to the existing national register, recently under international attack for falling standards and allowing transfer of dubiously maintained vessels into its books (40,44,49,51).

Figure 10
EuroAfrica Fleet as on 31st December 1996

Ro-ro vessels	Flag	Year	Capacity	DWT	Passengers
Amber	NIS	1993	1278m	5390	12
Elbląg	POL	1980	865m	4140	12
Inowrocław	POL	1980	1403m	8700	12
Puck	POL	1980	786m	4140	12
Rail-car ferries					
Jan Sniadecki	CYP	1980	1175m	5580	67
Mikolaj Kopernik	CYP	1980	650m	2500	46
Semi-container vessels					
Kwidzyn	POL	1974	134TEU	3860	6
Lębork	POL	1975	134TEU	3860	6
Wejherowo	POL	1975	134TEU	3860	6
Conventional vessels					
Agat	CYP	1981	422thcuft	9290	6
Wladysław Lokietek	VCT	1972	481thcuft	11625	6
Zygmunt August	VCT	1971	481thcuft	11625	6
Zabrze	POL	1971	365thcuft	7000	6
Zambrów	POL	1969	365thcuft	7000	6
Zawichost	POL	1970	365thcuft	7000	6
Rubin	CYP	1981	422thcuft	9290	6
Rail/Passenger/Freight Ferry					
Polonia	BAH	1995	2350m	7200	920
(50% owned with Z.P.S.A.)					

Source: EuroAfrica, 1996

Trades

1996 total figures for trades were the same as for 1995. Details of loadings over recent years are given in Figures 11, 12 and 13 below. They reflect a consistently growing figure of traffic but particularly on the UK line, with the smallest growth (some 0.32% from 1994 to 1995) on the West Africa line. Between the same two years, export cargoes rose by 6.9% in comparison with import growth of 5.4%. The most significant rise in the volume of exports occurred on the UK and West Africa lines, and the most significant for imports on the Finnish line. Some 30240 trucks and road trailers were carried during 1995. The figures below exclude traffic on the "Polonia", Unity Line operation between Świnoujście and Ystad in Sweden.

Figure 11
Outward Cargo (volume in '000 tonnes)

Volume	1991	1992	1993	1994	1995
Polish Foreign Trade	337.2	350.7	267.4	349.8	403.3
Transit	64.9	53.4	28.4	323.6	290.3
Cross trade	51.0	74.4	85.2	66.5	97.4
TOTAL	493.1	478.5	381.0	739.9	791.0

Figure 12
Inward cargo (volume in '000 tonnes)

Volume	1991	1992	1993	1994	1995
Polish Foreign Trade	125.6	148.4	186.8	328.1	328.7
Transit	52.3	62.0	103.8	361.1	326.6
Cross Trade	67.9	83.9	94.3	86.8	76.2
TOTAL	245.8	294.3	384.9	776.0	731.5

Figure 13
Total Cargo (volume in '000 tonnes)

Volume	1991	1992	1993	1994	1995
Polish Foreign Trade	502.8	499.1	454.2	677.9	732.0
Transit	117.2	115.4	132.2	684.7	616.9
Cross Trade	118.9	158.3	179.5	153.3	173.6
TOTAL	738.9	772.8	765.9	1515.9	1522.5

Source Tables 11, 12, 13: EuroAfrica 1996

These Figures indicate one or two interesting developments in traffic over the five year period. Firstly, the dramatic increase in all figures from 1994 reflects the inclusion of trucks and trailers in the data. However, even neglecting this new data, the traffic volume figures have been increasing steadily since 1991 in almost all sectors, reflecting the upturn in the Polish economy in general. Secondly, is the notable decline in outward transit cargo (again ignoring the truck and trailer input) which may reflect the changing pattern of movement of goods from central Europe through German ports (e.g. Hamburg and Bremerhaven) rather than the traditional pattern of the old CMEA days using Polish ports and services. For some reason, inward transit cargo appears to continue growing. Thirdly, rather surprisingly, cross trade levels remain relatively constant, at a time when the need for alternative hard currency income would have been paramount, to replace the lost, guaranteed CMEA trade.

In 1997, the company operated the following groups of liner services.

(1) UK Line. Gdynia-Felixstowe-Hull-Gdynia.

This is a weekly roll on/roll off service operated by the m/s Inowrocław until recently (see Figure 10) and co-ordinated with the service provided by UBC of the United Kingdom based and owned, Andrew Weir Shipping Group. This co-operation recommenced following a number of years of straight competition, in February 1995 whereby both partners agreed to create a freight/cost container pool and to promote joint freight policy whilst maintaining at the same time, a separate marketing organisation. The previous independent arrangement had been abandoned due to the falling cargo levels, particularly on the EuroAfrica vessel, but following the agreement, there was an immediate increase in trade that has led to the present pattern of services.

UBC also serves Gdynia, Felixstowe and Hull in a similar pattern and frequency. Trade in 1995, for example, increased by some 49% representing the greatest growth of traffic on any line operated by EuroAfrica.

(2) Ireland Line. Szczecin-Dublin.

This is a semi-container service operating every two weeks utilising the m/v Wejherowo (see Figure 10). Trade is limited on this route as a result of the fairly low level of economic activity between the Republic of Ireland and Poland. Recent results have shown a small increase in traffic, particularly in imports of containerised cargo, thus reducing the need to reposition empty boxes. Occasionally, the service also diverts to carry additional cargoes including recently, the example of 30000 tons of cathodic copper from Szczecin to Rotterdam.

(3) Finland Lines. Gdynia - Helsinki - Kotka - Gdynia. Szczecin - Turku - Helsinki - Szczecin. Gdynia - Helsinki - Gdynia.

These services comprise three routes each with a dedicated ship - respectively m/v Puck and m/v Amber, joined by m/v Elbląg in 1995 to meet growing demand. Each provides roll on/roll off services on a weekly basis for trucks, trailers and containers. In recent years there has been substantial growth on these routes and they are a major contributor to the profits of EuroAfrica benefiting from the new and developing linkages with the countries of Scandinavia and links through Finland to Russia avoiding the problems inherent in road border crossings in the Baltic States, Belarus and the Kaliningrad enclave. Another significant factor was the withdrawal of the PZB Gdańsk - Helsinki service in 1995, diverting truck and trailer services to the EuroAfrica route. Recent traffic figures indicate some 370000 tons of cargo from 1995, increasing by 23% on the year 1994 which itself had seen dramatic growth. Areas of particular development included exports from Poland and transhipment cargo through Gdynia from Finland to West Africa using EuroAfrica's connecting services. From early 1997, a new development of the Finnish services has been provided by the Pol-Fin line between Gdynia and Helsinki and served by the "Amber" from EuroAfrica in conjunction with the "Ann Mari" of Finnish shipping operator Fin Carriers.

(4) West Africa Line. Szczecin - West European ports - Banjul (The Gambia) - Tema (Ghana) - Lagos (Nigeria).

This service is operated in loose collaboration with the state-owned Estonian Shipping Company (ESCO) and supported by six conventional vessels, in the range of 7000 to 11500 DWT and with limited accommodation for passengers. These ships include m/s Władysław Lokietek, m/s Zygmunt August, m/s Agat, m/s Rubin, m/s Zambrów and m/s Zawichost. Various additional ports in west Europe, the Canary Islands and West Africa may be included in the schedules on inducement. Frequency of sailings varies from one to three a month. In recent years, carryings on the West Africa Line have been steady although there have been noticeable problems in the trades with Nigeria due to local political and economic difficulties in that region. Vessel round trip times have reduced due to increased efficiency in Nigerian ports as a consequence of the reduced demand. Financial problems, particularly those of extracting payments from the West African market, have caused a series of erratic phases in demand that have continued for some years. The trade is also seasonal in that the main Nigerian export involved remains cocoa.

(5) Ferry services.

EuroAfrica is involved in the ferry services between Ystad (Sweden) and Świnoujście (Poland) using one passenger ferry with limited freight facilities ("Polonia") half owned by Z.P.S.A. of Szczecin (effectively PZM) in a joint venture, and the m/f Nikolaj Kopernik and m/f Jan Sniadecki, both essentially freight vessels with very limited passenger accommodation (46 and 67 passengers respectively). Three sailings daily are operated from each port. The services by the jointly owned "Polonia" and the other two ferries are marketed under the name of Unity Line, a service which it was intended would originally include PZB as well, but which, as we shall examine in the chapter on PZB succumbed to the political difficulties within the industry at the time. The ferry services of EuroAfrica underwent considerable revision in 1995 with the introduction of the "Polonia", on the 1st June resulting in an increase in cargo and passenger carrying capabilities which increases in demand in 1994 suggested were necessary. EuroAfrica believe that there is an urgent need to consolidate the ferry services provided within Poland - and this possibly reflects the overcapacity on the market in general that the introduction of the "Polonia" in 1995 did nothing to constrain. This is a topic which we shall return to again in a later section concerning PZB. EuroAfrica would appear to favour some sort of agreement with PZB, which might even involve taking them over possibly through the privatisation process announced in 1997 for the latter company. The long term aim would be to retain the few large scale and modern assets PZB owns - e.g. the port of Kołobrzeg and the "Boomerang" high speed catamaran acquired in 1997 - and the Świnoujście ferry terminal, and scrapping all the rest including most vessels. Returns in the Polish ferry market are not adequate - and worsened by the invasion of Lion Ferry (Stena Line) recently and the creation of a single mega-carrier through Unity Line with Z.P.S.A. would allow sufficient reinvestment to occur. One organisation could combine all the threads of passenger and freight demands, rail cars, tourism and duty-free services, the latter growing in significance as the European Union removes the opportunity for duty-free shopping on intra-Union services in 1998/9 including those between Sweden, Germany, Denmark and Finland. However, there have been no discussions as yet and to quote EuroAfrica, "dialogue is difficult" with an operator tied down by Workers Councils, Trades Unions, old ships and high debts. Various suggestions have been put forward for the introduction of a fast ferry service on the Unity Line route but as yet, to no avail. The plans suggested in 1995 were to supplement the "Polonia" operations with a second hand craft carrying around 400 passengers and 100 cars - interestingly enough a time when EuroAfrica were complaining of overcapacity in the market. However, the whole project needs to be seen in the context of the continuing dispute between PZB and Unity Line and the local political environment that continues to exist, manifesting itself in 1997 in the PZB "Boomerang" affair. Unity Line remains an interesting, if confusing example of the modern Polish maritime industries. It is, for example not only a ship operating company in "private hands" - at least in Polish terms, but also a 50/50 joint venture between ex-state companies, and managed by Isle of Man based Polonia Line Ltd.

Equity investments

Along with most other interests in the Polish shipping industries, EuroAfrica and has become actively involved in taking equity investments in other companies as the process of privatisation and diversification continues within the sector. This complicates the process of attempting to understand the industry as a whole as well as the individual companies concerned as the complexity of holdings is becoming increasingly difficult to disentangle and changes with frequency and regularity. All we can attempt to do here is assess the situation as it stood in 1996, with the provision that the reader understands that changes are occurring all the time.

EuroAfrica Shipping Lines Company Limited (ESL) retained equity interest in the following companies as at 1st January, 1996:

(1) 99.9% BALFER - Limassol, Cyprus. Shipowner company. Owner of "Jan Sniadecki" ferry.

(2) 50.0% POLONIA LINE Co. Ltd. - Isle of Man investment company. This company is a joint venture of ESL and Żegluga Polska S.A. in order to finance the construction of the "Polonia".

(3) 50.0% UNITY LINE Co. Ltd. - Szczecin ship-owning company set up as a joint venture of ESL and Żegluga Polska S.A. to provide for the operation of "Polonia" and the two remaining ferries on the route.

(4) 49.0% POL LEVANT Shipping Lines Ltd. - Gdynia based ship-operating company. This company is EuroAfrica's main trading partner for trans-shipment cargoes.

(5) 34.0% POL-LINE AB - Ystad, Sweden based shipping agency company. The company acts as booking and port agents for the ESL operations to and from Świnoujście.

(6) 30.0% FIN-POL Shipping Ltd.- a general shipping agency company acting as agent for ESL services in Finland and as a marketing and sales organisation for the company.

(7) 24.0% PSAL Agencies NV - Antwerp based shipping agency. General agent in Belgium for all POL group companies and ESL.

(8) 22.0% POL-AGENT - Szczecin based forwarding and shipping agency company. The company provides agency services for all ESL vessels calling at Szczecin and irregularly for ESL vessels calling at Gdynia and Gdańsk. It also acts as booking agent for ESL and arranges door to door transport for cargoes within Poland.

(9) 22.0% POL-MARINE Ltd. - Gdynia based insurance brokers which emerged from the POL group restructuring and has taken over the business of the former insurance and claims departments of POL. By taking equity possession in this company, ESL has secured advantageous insurance and claims settlement assistance for its vessels.

(10) 22.0% DELFIN - Szczecin based house building company. Delfin has been set up to provide the personnel of its shareholding companies (including ESL) with housebuilding facilities.

More recently, EuroAfrica has taken an interest in Pekaes Speditor, the former state owned international trucking company, providing further inland, road based services. Further investments are planned. As yet they very largely involve companies whose primary activities are directly related to those of ESL, aiming to integrate the needs and ambitions of both to mutual benefit.

Future plans

EuroAfrica see themselves as a dynamic company and the new face of Polish shipping. They have a number of definite plans which they are directing towards maintaining that position and developing their role further in the coming years.

Quite openly they admit that the age of the majority of vessels that they operate means that the renewal of the fleet is an urgent requirement. With the exception in particular of the "Polonia", the rest of the fleet is becoming in need of replacement and the first set of vessels to be considered will be those that serve the West African ports. The plan here has been to replace the four conventional vessels on these routes with three or four new vessels or second-hand vessels in the range of 10-12000 DWT. The first steps towards their replacement took place in late 1997.

In addition, the continued growth on the Poland - Finland trade has now exceeded the capacity of the available vessels and there is an urgent need to review the availability of space and to restructure services to ensure a sufficient provision for the market. This may involve increased tonnage, or may simply be resolved, at least for the moment, through organisational changes.

EuroAfrica has also established recently, a new office in Gdynia which will now concentrate its activities and developments in providing intermodal transport services.

Another new activity that will require considerable development is the diversification of the company's business into wholesale trading within the area of imported consumer goods and the fish and fish product market. This diversification of interests should help to provide a more stable base for the industry and also to ensure that the company is less exposed to the periodic difficulties and downturns faced by shipping in general world-wide.

Meanwhile, the company has moved towards the achievement of ISO9002 since 1995 and in the process negotiated the transfer of the Polish Ocean Line crews that it used, into the EuroAfrica company so that sufficient control of standards could be ensured. ISO9002 was granted in 1996 and during that year the first ISO9002 certificates were awarded to EuroAfrica vessels beginning with the ferry fleet, and then moving on successively to roll on/roll off and other vessels.

Finally, EuroAfrica has plans concerning diversification into the land market. At present they own all their own land and buildings in Szczecin - in fact the first company to achieve freehold ownership in the city since the political changes. The aim is to extend this ownership to neighbouring sites and to go on to develop the site (and others) in partnership with a developer who would carry much of the risk, unlike the financially difficult moves that PZM underwent in their redevelopment of sites in Szczecin.

Discussion

EuroAfrica Line throws up a number of interesting issues in the development of Polish shipping and in particular in the transition from the old command economy and system of centralised management and the introduction of more free market principles.

The ownership structure of the new company presents some interesting characteristics but especially so in terms of the level of privatisation that it truly represents. Certainly within the eyes of Polish business law and the Commercial Code, there is no doubt that EuroAfrica is a private company with private ambitions, objectives, rules and a private structure and organisation. However, close examination of the various stakeholders in the company may suggest other conclusions - and certainly other influences - in that a large number remain heavily influenced by the state and are, in some cases, effectively state organisations. Potentially in this group are included the various port authorities with an interest and the Polish Ocean Lines umbrella group. Any analysis of EuroAfrica's activities must remain aware of the potential for at least state influence within the organisation, even if formally there is no state owner of the company. Admittedly, however, the role of the state may well now be lessening as the part played by Polish Ocean Lines declines from its near half ownership to one of only 27% (and further in December 1997, although the investment transfer was to PZM, also state still owned) and that of other private companies increases. Once again, however, it should be noted that these private companies include Polcontainer - the ex-POL company, PZM the still state owned bulk shipping company and Pekaes, the ex-state owned trucking company. Although these private owners are often reconstituted state companies in the private sector, they in turn remain heavily involved with state interests. Employee ownership continues to decrease as well, as the larger investors start to dominate.

It was also noted earlier, and deserves repeating here, how the proportion of POL direct ownership had decreased but at the same time the increase that has occurred in POL filial company stakes, in a sense just transferring the holding between members of the group. One clear benefit in all this to EuroAfrica is the business relationship that still exists with a large and well connected client base; one drawback, the poor and old fashioned image of the old POL empire.

The state of the vessels owned remains a major concern of the company. Only the half share of the "Polonia" can be described as a modern vessel - and in this case a very modern vessel - with most others ageing rapidly and in some need of replacement in the near future. This is not going to be easy as the revenues on most of the conventional shipping lines - in particular the West African route - are inadequate. The trades to the UK and to Finland are now prospering and here there is more hope of replacements in the near future. EuroAfrica does not, however, give any indication of withdrawing from the West African run despite the growing financial crisis. Traditional pursuits 'of carrying passengers on all freight routes remain in place and interestingly, are currently being investigated by competitors on the UK-Poland run as a way of diversifying activities and increasing revenue.

Growth in cargoes has been substantial since the early 1990s although it appears also to have stabilised recently. Particularly successful areas of trade have been in terms of transit cargo - largely with the states of the Former Soviet Union - with moderate growth in cross-trade work and that for the domestic economy. This domination of FSU work is a trend in many parts of the Polish maritime economy and one that is set to continue as the Baltic ports attempt to target these markets. Outward cargo movements have shown much less growth than inward, although from a much higher base.

Perhaps one of the most interesting areas stems from the activities of EuroAfrica in the "Polonia" operation and its continued collaboration with PZM. We shall return to this issue in some detail in the section discussing Polska Żegluga Bałtycka (PZB), but a number of points of interest would be appropriate to be noted here.

In particular, it represents an unusual combination of ex-state owned operators (EuroAfrica and PZM) coming together to form a joint venture in a market in which neither were particular expert and without the co-operation of PZB who were, of course, the monopoly provider of ferry services under the old regime. The absence of PZB is a result of a combination of political and economic disagreements that continue to influence operations and policy within the maritime sector as the old state companies turn to the private sector.

Meanwhile the formation of Unity Line - the new joint venture private company - and the purchase of "Polonia" through an off-shore Isle of Man company is representative of the new Polish maritime sector. Bahamian flagged and built overseas, on the one hand it offers unrivalled comfort on the route between Ystad and Świnoujście, but on the other, is reputed to be heavily underused and losing large sums of money. Partly, at least because of the associated political intrigue, and partly because of commercial confidentiality it is difficult to be sure of anything, but undoubtedly competition on the Swedish market is fierce, relations with PZB poor and at times, commercial considerations may have come second to those of politics.

Equally as interesting and thoroughly complex are the range of joint ventures and equity investments made by EuroAfrica in a series of off-shore financial companies, diversifications and overseas representatives - all of which are typical of the new Poland but which were unimaginable prior to the economic, social and political changes of the late 1980s. The continuing moves towards flagging out and the decline of the Polish registered fleet are both reflected here in the role of companies set up in Cyprus and the Isle of Man. The complexities of ownership are apparent here as well with EuroAfrica appearing to be attempting to make life as difficult as possible for the analyst with a combination of overseas stakes, semi-state interests and combinations of involvement in a wide variety of small and specific companies.

Conclusions

EuroAfrica continues to move on. There are plans for land investments and further diversification plus involvement in inter-modal transport and possibly new markets. Underlying this process of change is that of privatisation without which nothing would have occurred and EuroAfrica would have remained locked within its world as the Szczecin based subsidiary of the Polish Ocean Lines Group. Although this privatisation is peculiarly Polish in its characteristics its results are beginning to be seen and EuroAfrica represents a successful venture in the free-market that receives little support from the state, certainly in direct terms.

It faces problems still - in particular the need for reinvestment in vessels and the economic problems associated with their finance particularly with the company saddled with the debts of the "Polonia" venture. It is not impossible that EuroAfrica will attempt to buy a stake in the privatisation of PZB - announced during 1997 - and thus to expand its ferry interests and to remove a competitor from the market place. PZB will not welcome this move following the continued political problems that exist, but EuroAfrica may see it as a way of further market consolidation, diversification and a way of acquiring assets (e.g. the port of Kołobrzeg) that could form the basis for vessel renewal.

Further developments at EuroAfrica are assured for a company with the longest experience in the maritime sector of exposure to the rigours of privatisation and one that displays all the typical characteristics of that process in modern Poland.

Polska Żegluga Bałtycka
(Polferries)

Introduction

Polska Żegluga Bałtycka (PZB), otherwise commonly known as Polish Baltic Shipping and trading as "Polferries", is the smallest of the three state owned shipping companies in Poland inherited from the times before the transformation of the late 1980s. As we shall see later on in this chapter, PZB has responsibilities in the coastal shipping, ferry and ports sector and as such is rather less well defined in its activities than those which were designated for PZM and Polish Ocean Lines. This rather ill-defined specification is linked with its eccentric head quarters location in Kołobrzeg, almost midway along the Baltic coast between Gdynia and Szczecin and thus far from the major maritime centres of Poland. The company presents a fascinating picture of an enterprise that was invented by the old regime and which today still suffers from the artificial environment in which it works and the unusual structures and relationships that surround it.

A brief history

The state owned enterprise of PZB was set up by the Ministry of Foreign Trade and Maritime Economy on the 31st January 1976 as a shipping company with the functions of:

(1) the organisation of passenger/tourist traffic including coastal shipping services;

(2) hotel, catering, tourist and leisure services for domestic and foreign tourists;

(3) maritime cargo shipping using coastal and inland waterways;

(4) organisation and operation of port services in Kołobrzeg, Ustka, Łeba and Darłowo;

(5) agency services for all the activities noted above;

(6) repair and building works for the company's needs.

From the very start, and even before its formation, PZB was faced with problems. In almost all ways, it was an artificial company in that its creation was at the insistence of the state and resisted heavily by the existing shipping companies of Polish Ocean Lines and PZM. It is widely rumoured that the state in 1976 wanted to achieve two things through creating PZB - to support the ailing economy of the Kołobrzeg region; and to satisfy strong political factions in the region. At the meeting called to create the company, it is reported that the Minister threatened to dismiss all the senior personnel of both Polish Ocean Lines and PZM if they would not agree with the proposal, including the divestment of a number of ships to PZB, without compensation. The result of all this was predictable - the oldest ships were transferred, the shipping company is located in a curious location, and most importantly, the resentment felt by Polish Ocean Lines and PZM remains to this day. More of that later.

To co-ordinate and organise the activities which it was delegated, PZB was set up with four branches of activities, viz.:

- tourist (including ferry services), hotel and catering;
- small tramping;
- port services;
- repair and building.

Initially, PZB began activities in the hotel construction business, but in true style of a company continuously dogged by controversy since its formation, the state insisted that the majority of this work and the ownership of the proposed hotels should be transferred to the state owned travel company "Orbis". Two hotels were built under PZB's auspices in Gdańsk and Gdynia, yet subsequently also transferred to Orbis.

Ferry shipping operations have always been the major activity of the company but did not really begin until the forced transfer of vessels from Polish Ocean Lines of Gryf, Skandynawia, Wawel and Wilonanów passenger ferries, and Goplana, Krasnal, Nimfa, Świetlik and Rusałka freight vessels; Hajnówka, Ruciane, Barlinek, Ina, Ner, Soła, Krutynia, Orla and Odra from PZM; and the ferry terminals in Gdańsk and Świnoujście from the respective port authorities. The first PZB vessel to sail was the Ruciane on the 10th May, 1976. This inheritance was characterised by old and outdated equipment and accompanied by the absence of a capital base for PZB - which made for difficulties from the start. These difficulties remain apparent today.

In the late 1970s, PZB expanded into a number of services running between Poland, Denmark, Sweden and even the United Kingdom and during this period acquired and disposed of a number of vessels including the purchase of a new ferry from the Szczecin shipyard in 1979, named "Pomerania".

The 1980s were testing times for the enterprise, and PZB faced severe financial difficulties that matched those of Poland as a whole. The conditions at PZB were exacerbated by the poor infrastructural condition of the company's equipment, in combination with the lack of financial resources, a limited ability to earn hard currency through international transport services, and the severe political crisis within Poland during the early 1980s including the imposition of martial law which prompted economic restrictions by west European countries. The Ministry of Maritime Economy as a result, commenced preliminary liquidation of the company and prompted the sale of "Pomerania" and "Silesia" to PZM including their large, accumulated debts. This stemmed what had looked like inevitable liquidation and this process of divestment of ships continued with the sale of "Gryf "and "Skandynawia". Meanwhile, between 1981 and 1991, "Pomerania" and "Silesia" were chartered to foreign owners to work in the Mediterranean and " Rogalin" to work between Eire, Iceland, the United Kingdom and Norway.

Throughout the 1980s, PZB recovered its position and reached a peak of ferry development in 1989 when services were operated between Świnoujście and Ystad, Copenhagen, Nynäshamn and Travemünde; between Gdańsk and Travemünde, Riga, Ronne, Helsinki and Nynäshamn; and between Helsinki and Visby. Since then, some of the ferry services have been rationalised and modified as we shall see later, the port of Kołobrzeg has been partially modernised and a new ferry terminal at Świnoujście has been opened.

PZB suffered considerably during the 1990s and in particular in 1993 when the composition of the board of the company changed some three times and losses for the year amounted to around 80bn old złotys (approximately US$3m, 1997). Between 1989 and 1991, interest liabilities rose from 1.1% of earnings to around 55%. This was followed by the cancellation of a new building for a 1000 passenger ferry and a partial restructuring of the company with the loss of 400 jobs. Since then, the situation has improved with figures for 1995 of a turnover of 138.8m złoty (US$51.41m) (43, 48).

Company structure

The structure of PZB has remained remarkably stable over the years since it was formed but with minor modifications occurring in the 1990s, as noted above, when the "building section" was liquidated as the first stages of moves towards privatisation were taken. At the same time, responsibility for the port of Darłowo, Ustka and Łeba were transferred to their local municipalities. Currently (late 1997), the company employs around 1800 staff altogether, of which 1200 are sea-going, 170 work at the Świnoujście Terminal, 30 at the Gdańsk Terminal, 355 are administrative staff at Kołobrzeg, 100 work in the travel offices and five are port administrators at Kołobrzeg (63). The latter is a small number because the majority of activities in the port are now carried out by private sector companies. PZB itself, does not undertake port operations.

Company activities can be divided into three sections:

(1) Ports. Responsibilities here include the terminals at Świnoujście and at Gdańsk and those of the Port of Kołobrzeg, concentrated on the eastern side of the Parsęta River. The remainder of the latter port is operated privately.

The Świnoujście terminal serves both PZB vessels and their competitors in the form of Unity Line (jointly owned by PZM and EuroAfrica). Gdańsk Terminal serves PZB vessels only. The Świnoujście Terminal has a long and chequered history particularly in terms of the very recent developments. Up to 1997, this redevelopment had taken some eight years and remained unfinished, although the final stages are now in sight. The terminal was partially opened in 1994.

Some 20% of the cost of the development has been funded by PZB, which in itself is unusual in Poland where traditionally, port infrastructure has been the responsibility of the port authority or the state. The remaining 80% has been funded directly by the state whose promises of money, and particularly its timing, has been rather unpredictable resulting in the delays. Commonly only 70% of the annual budget has been provided and this in turn has caused an erratic progress of development leaving much to be desired. Services are operated from the terminal to Ystad in Sweden by Unity Line, on a once daily basis and to Malmö (Sweden) by ship twice daily and by high speed catamaran twice daily, to Copenhagen (Denmark) by ship six times a week and to Rønne (Denmark) by ship, daily in summer only. A new freight service was also started in 1996 to Aabenraa in Sweden.

Details of the Gdańsk Terminal are outlined in the chapter on the Port of Gdańsk and will not be repeated here. PZB is the sole user (and owner) and services are provided by ship to Oxelösund in Sweden weekly and to Nynäshamn (also in Sweden) up to once daily.

The port of Kołobrzeg covers some 22 hectares and is situated on the Parsęta River in the province of Koszalin and lies between Gdynia and Szczecin on the Baltic Coast. It is the fifth largest commercial seaport in Poland after the international ports of Gdańsk, Gdynia, Szczecin and Świnoujście and its activities are dominated by those of PZB whose headquarters are in the port area. Curiously enough however, and as a result of the chequered history of the company, PZB operate no ferries from the port and only a limited number of coastal freighters. Ships of 75 metres length, 13 metres breadth and 4.5 metres draught can be accommodated. 1996 figures for cargo traffic indicate that some 61900 tonnes of general cargo and 61100 tonnes of grain passed through the port accompanied by limited quantities of timber (14000 tonnes) and other bulk commodities (30000 tonnes) giving a total throughput of 154400 tonnes for the year. A very small quantity of liquid cargo was also processed. Some 5000 sq. metres of warehouses are available along with 55000 sq. metres of open storage yards and a 6000 tonne grain silo. There are 11 mobile cranes with lifting capacities of up to 16 tonnes. Around 160000 tonnes of cargo is anticipated for 1997.

Plans exist to develop the port entrance to accommodate vessels of up to 100 metres length, and to attract a service to and from the Danish island of Bornholm which lies only 50 miles from Kołobrzeg.

(2) Shipping. This can be divided into three parts.

Ferry services form the major activity of the company and have been outlined in the previous section. Until 1995, the services to Sweden and Denmark were augmented by a regular service from Gdańsk to Helsinki but this was withdrawn by PZB due to lack of demand. 1997 revisions have been dominated by the introduction of the fast ferry "Boomerang" to which we shall return in a subsequent section. All ferry activities have been subject to increasing competition from Unity lines in the west and Lion Ferries (Stena) in the east. This issue we shall also return to later. Fleet details are contained in Figure 14.

Tramp shipping includes the operation of a series of small coasters and short sea ships. In total there are eight vessels of which some four are on long term charter until the year 2000/2001 to the Fast organisation of Belgium operating between various locations on the continent to the United Kingdom, Denmark, Norway and Sweden. Operations are confined to the North Sea and the Baltic. Details of all eight vessels are given in Figure 14. Commodities carried are dominated by various bulk cargoes and additionally some general cargo and containers. Each of the vessels have collapsible bridges and a shallow draught thus enabling them to navigate inland waterways and reach the interior of Europe in Belgium, The Netherlands and the United Kingdom. They operate from both Kołobrzeg and Szczecin. The ships are owned by a series of subsidiary companies which in turn are owned either 100 or 99% by PZB. These companies include Grey Sky Limited and Blue Sky Limited of Cyprus and Sail Right Company of Liberia with all the benefits of financial accessibility that this brings. Temporarily some of them remain under the Polish flag as a legal requirement but are likely to be transferred to that of

Figure 14
PZB Fleet 1997

Vessel	Flag	DWT	Type	Built
Silesia	PL	10553*	Pass ferry	1979
Pomerania	PL	10550*	Pass ferry	1978
Nieborów	PL	8697*	Pass ferry	1973
Rogalin	PL	10241*	Pass ferry	1972
Ner	PL	1264	Gen cargo	1988
Sola	PL	1264	Gen cargo	1988
Fast Ann	PL	1999	Gen cargo	1980
Fast Catrien	PL	1999	Gen cargo	1980
Fast Filip	PL	1999	Gen cargo	1980
Fast Sim	PL	1678	Gen cargo	1980
Rusałka II	PL	2060	Bulk	1991
Nimfa II	PL	2060	Bulk	1991
Parsęta	PL	1029	Freight ferry	1970
Boomerang	BAH	346	HS Catamaran	1997

* GRT

Source: PZB, 1997

Vanuatu as soon as possible. In a later section we shall examine the issue of privatisation but for the minute it is worth noting that all the vessels will be flagged out following privatisation essentially for financial reasons and in particular the need to raise capital for vessel renewal. The current Polish commercial law regime that places ships under the domestic flag and thus the banks that have provided finance for their purchase, fourth after the state, crew and social security in terms of creditors, makes domestic flagging unacceptable.

PZB also conducts its own maritime operations and thus works actively on the tramp market using two small coasters (the "Ner" and the "Sola") running between the Baltic, the North Sea and up the Rhine as far as Duisburg in Germany. Two larger bulkers are used into and out of Kołobrzeg in similar markets ("Rusałka II" and "Nimfa II").

(3) Sea travel offices. These are essentially travel agencies which sell primarily ferry tickets (for all operators), rail tickets and organise cruises and other leisure trips using PZB vessels. Ten offices are located across Poland at Warsaw, Poznań, Łódź, Szczecin, Gdynia, Kraków, Wrocław, Świnoujście

and Kołobrzeg, and one each in Sweden (Oxelösund) and Denmark (Copenhagen).

Market share and levels

Figures 15, 16 and 17 give an indication of PZB's place within the ferry market structure operating into and out of Poland in recent years. The Figures reveal a number of interesting trends which can be directly related to the restructuring of the Polish maritime marketplace and more specifically, the Baltic ferry marketplace. PZB claims to have 1% of the total Baltic seaborne traffic and 60% of all Polish trade.

There is clear evidence that PZB has an important market share of the passenger marketplace but lags behind Unity Line in the trucking sector into and out of southern Sweden. It is also clear that the entry of Unity Line into the market in competition with PZB has had serious implications for the latter who have lost a sizeable part of their market share to the new operator.

Figure 15
PZB traffic 1996 (annual total/average)

Traffic Type	Świn Copen	Świn Malmö	Gdańsk Oxel	Świn Rønne	Świn Aaben	TOTAL /Ave
Passengers	79034	206479	95371	6393	0	387277
Cars	9487	44722	19502	803	0	74514
Trucks	7590	10433	1722	18	550	20313
Voyages	359	620	201	22	46	1247
Pass/voy	220	333	476	291	0	311
Cars/voy	26	72	97	37	0	60
Trucks/voy	21	17	9	1	12	16

Figure 16
PZB and Unity Line market shares 1995/1996

	Świn/Malmö (PZB)		Świn/Ystad (Unity)	
	1995	1996	1995	1996
Passengers	114477	206479 (57%)	78961	156333 (43%)
Cars	29675	44722 (54%)	20837	37662 (46%)
Trucks	11781	10433 (18%)	26690	48161 (82%)

Figure 17
Poland - Sweden ferry routes, 1995/1996. All operators.

	Passengers		Cars		Trucks	
	1995	1996	1995	1996	1995	1996
PZB Malmö	245071	206479	61959	44722	17178	10433
PZB Oxel.	76056	95371	15398	19509	1213	1722
Unity Line	137289	157910	33285	39425	40159	48025
Lion Ferry	94268	141003	14685	23585	6500	9200
TOTAL	552684	600763	125327	127241	65050	69380

Source: PZB, 1997.

Lion Ferry, the Stena owned operator running daily between Gdynia and Karlskrona in southern Sweden also presents a growing threat in all sectors and must pose a sizeable problem to PZB from eastern Poland.

Overall, all sectors of the market are growing as a direct result of the entry of Sweden (and Finland) into the European Union and the liberalisation of the Polish marketplace - both factors encouraging a growth in freight and leisure traffic. An additional benefit stemming from these trends is the likely growth in traffic with the loss of duty free facilities on intra-European Union sailings from 1999 - in particular from those between Germany and Sweden at present. PZB looks forward to great growth in this market, at least until Poland gains their own membership some time in the medium term. However, competition as a result, is increasing and we shall see in the following section how PZB have reacted to the situation in general in terms of route structuring and vessel refurbishment, renewal and replacement. One trend that does not emerge from the data here is that PZB made a profit in 1993 and 1995 - the last available figures - in the latter year of 2m złotys (US$620,000). This stemmed from a turnover of 150m złoty in 1995, which continued at around the same level in 1996.

Unity Line

The recent activities of PZB and its strategy within the marketplace has been determined largely by two issues. Firstly that of the impending privatisation of the company - which we shall return to in some detail in a later section - and the second issue which we shall deal with now is that of the competition on PZB's traditional, main market between Świnoujście and southern Sweden, presented by the emergence of Unity Line. This latter issue is one fraught with political over and undertones and one which has had major implications for the activities and policy of PZB in recent years (29, 60).

Unity Line was established in July 1994 by its two shareholders - Żegluga Polska SA (owned entirely by Polska Żegluga Morska of Szczecin) and EuroAfrica as a private shipping company operating ferry services between western Poland and southern Sweden. Originally, the intention was to include PZB within the ownership group, but following a series of acrimonious discussions, PZB pulled out of the arrangement resenting the intrusion of PZM and POL in their traditional passenger markets. Since then they have competed directly within the market although PZB quickly moved their operations from Ystad to Malmö when Unity entered into an agreement with the former port. This caused even further problems for PZB when the transfer took place earlier than agreed with PZB's representative in Sweden - Pol Line - which as a consequence was left with no service to represent in the port. Subsequent rulings in court led to a substantial fine for PZB.

In 1995, Unity Line started operating in the ferry marketplace out of Świnoujście with three ships (see Figure 18). Two were freight vessels (truck and rail) inherited from EuroAfrica - the "Jan Śniadecki" and the "Mikołaj Kopernik" and the other was the real problem in the early negotiations with PZB - the newly constructed "Polonia". All three vessels are deployed between Świnoujście and Ystad in Sweden in direct competition with the PZB operations which, as we have seen, were transferred to Malmö and Copenhagen. "Polonia" operates one service daily in each direction between the two ports.

"Polonia" was a contentious issue from the start as it represented a massive increase in capacity in the market and a very expensive investment. It was intended that PZB's existing ferry operations would be reduced to allow for the introduction of "Polonia", but due to the failure to reach agreement this has not occurred - and in fact, this was one of the reasons why it did not occur. The result now is intense competition and sizeable over tonnaging and over capacity.

"Polonia" is a rail/passenger/truck/car ferry which is managed by the Isle of Man based Polonia Line Ltd through the 50/50 joint venture noted earlier. Costing some US$70m, it is registered in the Bahamas for good financial reasons and was built in Norway to the highest safety, environmental and passenger comfort standards in the world. It has a capacity of 1000 passengers, is crewed by 82 officers and seafarers and has been designed specifically for the route.

PZB failed to reach agreement on becoming a partner in the operation of Unity Line for three reasons -

(1) Financially, it looked like a risky venture particularly with respect to the "Polonia" venture;

Figure 18
Unity Line fleet

Vessel	Flag	Capacity	Year
Jan Śniadecki	CYP	5583DWT	1988
Mikołaj Kopernik	PL	2350DWT	1974
Polonia	BAH	1000 pass/trucks/ rail cars/cars	1995

Source: Author

(2) They were offered only a 30% share of the company, as a reflection of their share of the market. This they found unacceptable; and

(3) They also found it unacceptable to give up their shipping interests for the benefit of the company overall.

It is also likely that long term animosity over the foundation of PZB from PZM and Polish Ocean Lines (representing EuroAfrica) interests had some impact in the negotiations over Unity Line although it is very hard to be certain of this.

"Polonia" was actually a replacement ship for the PZM owned and operated freight ferry "Hevelius" which sank in the Baltic Sea. According to PZM it represented a diversification into the passenger market to boost the strength and flexibility of the company, thus spreading risks. PZB's view of this is that PZM already operated well over 100 vessels and one new passenger ferry would make little if any difference to the company's exposure to market fluctuations.

"Polonia" is by far the best physical manifestation of the free market concept applied to Polish shipping and there is some serious resistance to the full application of liberalisation in this way and in a market traditionally secure and reliable for the existing operators. PZB believe that the state should have intervened to prevent investment in the new vessel - and thus to have prevented the overcapacity that now exists - in part at least to have protected PZB as it approaches privatisation. The state's view was that it was a private venture and as such could not be prevented. In fact no pressure was applied at all upon the companies involved as far as can be determined at this stage.

Unity Line continues to operate on the route with the loadings we noted earlier in Figures 16 and 17 . What is particularly notable is the market share of trucks carried by the line - remember that two of the three vessels they operate are freight only - and the minority share they have of the southern Sweden passenger and car traffic. Although this share is rising, compared to that of PZB where the share is falling, it remains a minority and represents low loadings per voyage - PZB's estimate for average passenger loadings is as low as 185 per voyage (capacity 1000) averaged over the whole year. With a substantial debt associated with the ship - again estimated at US$30000 a day excluding operating costs - this suggests a severe financial burden on the two joint owners. In that sense PZB's decision not to join may have been justified. More of this later.

Lion Ferries

Lion Ferries is a part of the Stena organisation based in Sweden and as such represents one of the few shipping competitors in Poland that have invaded the market from outside (19). Commencing operations in 1995 when they took over at very short notice from the bankrupt private Corona Line, they provide a once daily service between Gdynia and Karlskrona in Sweden in competition with the PZB operations between Gdańsk and Oxelösund/Nynäshamn, and before its withdrawal, limited competition with the PZB Gdańsk - Helsinki route. The vessel originally used was the comparatively small "Lion Prince" but due to improvements in the market this was replaced in June 1997 by the "Stena Europe". Both vessels have and do operate under the Polish flag and the "Stena Europe" has additional capacity to accommodate 1330 passengers and 420 cars.

Although loadings are not very high, the route is experiencing growth for the reasons noted earlier associated with Swedish EU membership and the liberalisation of the Polish economy. Between January and September 1997, passenger figures grew 30% to 151886 whilst truck units rose by 27.6% to 8215.

Lion's presence on the market has had a negative impact upon PZB in the Gdańsk/Gdynia area providing direct competition which has lowered PZB's loadings and forced the latter to adjust its service provision as we shall see in the next section. It is widely agreed, however, that Stena's plan in developing the Gdynia route is to gain a foot in the Polish market with ambitions of developing trade and traffic further. Part of this development process will occur at the end of 1997 with the abandonment of the Lion name and a reversion to the open Stena title. PZB clearly feel threatened by the mere existence of such a big competitor and apart from adjusting services and vessels also fear that their own privatisation might be eyed by Stena as another way into the Polish marketplace.

Fleet renewal, refurbishment and replacement, and service adjustment

The increased competition that PZB has faced in their traditional ferry marketplace symbolised by the "Polonia" affair and the invasion of Stena, has driven the company to respond in fleet renewal, replacement and the alteration of routes and services.

We have already noted how the Gdańsk - Helsinki route has been abandoned at least in part as a response to the Stena developments in the east, and this was accompanied by the readjustment of PZB services to Sweden from Gdańsk with the abandonment of the Karlskrona run and the adoption of new services to Nynäshamn and Aabenraa with better access to Stockholm and onward services to Finland. In addition to this there have been major changes in the western marketplace - i.e. from Świnoujście - in both vessels and services. The most significant changes took place from summer 1997 with the introduction of the high speed catamaran "Boomerang".

"Boomerang", constructed by Austal Ships of Australia originally as an option order from the German ferry company TT-Line, was delivered to PZB during May 1997 and entered service on the Świnoujście - Malmö route in June of the same year. Capable of 40 knots with a capacity of 700 passengers, 175 cars or 70 cars and 10 coaches, "Boomerang" was introduced by PZB to replace existing, ageing tonnage on the Swedish/western Poland corridor and to introduce a new element of competition with Unity Line prior to the build up to PZB's privatisation. It represents the fourth fast catamaran ferry operating in the Baltic since April 1996 (32, 59)

"Boomerang" was also bought at a low (but unspecified) cost as PZB acquired her from the constructors of the vessel who had a purchaser in line but which who subsequently dropped out. It is valued at US$41m. The vessel is Bahamian flagged, owned by a PZB owned company based in Cyprus for financial reasons and financed through a loan from the Bank Handłowy of Poland - in itself an interesting development as it represents the first domestic finance of a new vessel in Poland since the transformation of the economy. At present the service runs only once daily in each direction but plans are that by the summer of 1998, two return trips will be made plus an additional stop at Copenhagen. Aimed solely at the passenger/leisure market and thus directly against the "Polonia", "Boomerang" can take trucks but the manoeuvrability within the vessel is poor and thus there is no attempt to market this service. Trailers are not allowed due to similar but worse problems. PZB is thus attempting to compete directly with the "Polonia" service and has left the freight market to the existing Unity Line freight ferry services. Interestingly enough, Unity Line had announced in 1996, that it would be investing in a fast ferry service on the same market but no further signs of progress have been made.

A further major fleet development has been the substantial refurbishment of the "Pomerania", a 1978 passenger ferry vessel that has been used on the Świnoujście - south Sweden route (58). Prompted by the increasingly stringent safety standards in the ferry industry and the need to compete with the newly installed "Polonia" of Unity Line, PZB decided to refurbish the "Pomerania" rather than invest in a new vessel. The renewal has been substantial, reflected in the introduction of some 1200 tons of new steel (representing 83% replacement), complete replacement of all cabins and their fittings and replacement of two of the four ship's engines. The "Pomerania" is now allocated to the Świnoujście - Malmö route with the "Silesia" allotted to the Copenhagen route. "Silesia" is soon to be modernised at the Gdańska Stocznia Remontowa ship repair yard. For safety regulation reasons, the "Wiłanow" was sold.

Finally, as we have noted earlier, PZB have invested heavily in the Świnoujście Terminal as part of their marketing strategy for the corridor, raising the standard for this port facility to the highest in the region. Around three-quarters of the ten year annual investment of 250bn (old) złoty in the terminal has been provided by the state with the rest coming from PZB itself. Total investment costs are estimated at 1300bn (old) złoty.

Privatisation

PZB is now in the final stages of privatisation and as such, is likely to be the first of the three state owned shipping companies to pass into the private sector (46, 47, 50). Both PZM and Polish Ocean Lines have restructured in a way that has placed a number of subsidiaries into semi-private ownership, but neither have themselves been placed into fully private hands.

PZB was never set up like their two state partners following the changes of the late 1980s and the early 1990s. as they were established on the 31st December, 1992 as a fully, 100% owned, State Treasury Exclusive Company, with the option to be privatised in a capital rather than shareholding way - i.e. an "SA" company rather than a joint stock "Sp. z.o.o." company with shares owned by the state. This, in effect, placed them one further step down the road towards privatisation and is part of the reason why they are the first to move on.

Invitation for bidders was announced in January of 1997 with not less than 10% of the company to be acquired, and with a deadline of September for all bids to be made. It was clearly stated that a domestic purchaser would be preferred and that under Polish Commercial Law employees would receive up to 15% of free shares. Five % would be earmarked for the government programme to compensate former owners for property confiscated under the old Communist regime and a further 10% would be used to help finance the planned reform of the state social security scheme.

Fear of advances from overseas investors - and in particular Lion Ferry (Stena) which already has a presence in Poland, and TT Line which does not, has forced the state Treasury Ministry to indicate a domestic preference. Further state preference details indicate that a non-shipping, financial based investor would be most preferred, the latter in particular to put off a bid from PZM/EuroAfrica following the political turmoil over the "Polonia" affair.

By August of 1997, the message was that some 70% of PZB would be available as part of a batch of 20 imminent privatisations with the awards due to be announced very late that year. By late September, a number of undisclosed bidders had emerged although some news seeping out had revealed that one of the bids had come from a consortium, "Bałtyckie Konsorcjum Inwestycyjne", which included EuroAfrica, PZM, the shipyard Gdańska Stocznia Remontowa, Polish company Forin and the state insurer Warta. Interestingly the advice from the Treasury had not put off either EuroAfrica or PZM and depending how it was calculated, the majority of the ownership of prospective buyers remained with the state in some form or another. This is not untypical of the process of privatisation that continues in Poland generally at this time.

The whole issue of privatisation in PZB has been fraught with problems, not least because it is the first in the highly politicised shipping sector. However, more important in causing conflict has been the discrepancy in state ownership between the three state companies of PZM, Polish Ocean and PZB. The former two were set up as joint stock companies as we saw earlier and as such were administered by their primary owners - the Ministry of Maritime Economy. PZB was, as a commercial state company, administered by the Treasury. This conflict at ministerial level explains the difference in speed of privatisation between the companies, their different structural reforms and lays behind some of the decisions relating to investments in competing vessels (for example the "Boomerang" and the "Polonia") and the failure to reach agreement over the creation of Unity Line. Animosity between the companies, including EuroAfrica, and the openly expressed distaste by PZB to be sold to interests of PZM or Polish Ocean Lines are indications of the poor relationship that continues to exist.

Discussion

PZB presents a wide range of issues to discuss and provides a considerable number of good examples of the problems facing the Polish maritime industry and the political themes that underlie many of the decisions taken.

However, any discussion of the current position of PZB in the marketplace and their role within the Polish shipping industry has to begin with an appreciation of the way and circumstances in which the company was established in the 1970s and the effects of the decisions made then upon the subsequent progress that has been achieved.

PZB was not wanted by the rest of the state owned shipping industry - i.e. PZM and Polish Ocean Lines, who saw its creation as a political move which would lessen their importance and would create a diluted industry where their roles would be partly duplicated and certainly affected by the new company's presence. The specific reasons for its creation remain lost but undoubtedly smacked of a combination of political power - in that it would enable the creation, and thus reward, a new set of shipping company directors -. and poorly thought out ambitions of regional development in the Kołobrzeg area. There may well have also been an element of attempting to lessen the impact and power of the existing companies - but we have no evidence to prove this.

This was far from an auspicious start to the company, made worse by the Ministry insisting of the transfer of assets - mainly ships - to the new company from PZM and Polish Ocean Lines. The result was a fierce combination of resentment and anger that remains today. The poorest quality vessels were transferred and the under capitalised PZB had no possibilities to renew or replace these vessels quickly enough or to a quality that was likely to be sufficient. This vessel overhang remains today with only "Boomerang" and the refitted "Pomerania" having any claims to being modern.

However, worse was to follow. The highly extended talks to create the new ferry operator of Unity Line following liberalisation of the market, degenerated into further resentment and bad feeling. There is plenty of implied evidence to suggest that the two eventual owners - PZM and EuroAfrica (notably, a product of Polish Ocean and PZM) - had little intention of ever accommodating PZB as a full and true partner in the company. PZB thus refused to be involved and the ill feeling grew. This was extended further by what was seen by PZB as the failure of either the Finance or Maritime Ministry to intervene and prevent the creation of the new operator and thus to allow the over-capacity in the western Polish marketplace that now undoubtedly exists. PZB's view is that two state operators could have been persuaded, if not forced to abandon the idea of expanding tonnage out of Świnoujście on the basis of economic rationality. This was again given further expression by the impending privatisation of PZB, which was felt by the company to be damaged by the competitive approaches of Unity Line, supported by the state.

That leads us to the next area of interest/concern which stems from the privatisation and ownership issues that surround PZB. PZB was set up under the new liberalised shipping structure as a fully owned commercial company under the responsibility of the Treasury and with the prospect of capitalised privatisation - i.e. sold to another commercial concern or concerns rather than to the public through a share issue. The impact of this has been two fold. Firstly, the company has been little restructured prior to the privatisation moves which are now being made and unlike those that have taken place in either PZM or Polish Ocean Lines. This may have inhibited the progress of the company and certainly has not helped in its adaptation to the new commercial environment. Secondly, it has placed PZB into different ownership during the transition phase from that of PZM or Polish Ocean Lines. PZB has been effectively managed by the state Treasury whilst the latter two companies have been the responsibility of the Ministry of Maritime Economy. The rivalry between these two ministries is intense and the result appears to have been a political battle fought out in the scenario of privatisation of state shipping operators. Thus the Maritime Ministry has encouraged PZM and Polish Ocean to develop Unity Line in competition with PZB as a deliberate move to harm the latter as privatisation approaches and possibly even to facilitate the purchase of PZB by a consortium involving both or either of the other two. In late 1997 this scenario was beginning to emerge. Thus the uncomfortable role that PZB has always held in Kołolbrzeg, operating within an environment of animosity, might well come full circle in that their competitors will regain their markets, vessels and power through purchase of PZB.

The issue of competition also raises its head outside of the relationships between PZB, PZM and Polish Ocean Lines. The emergence of Lion Ferry, owned by Stena Lines of Sweden, in the east of Poland operating a daily service from Gdynia to Karlskrona in direct competition with PZB to Sweden, has created a fierce competitive environment which surprised PZB and has led to some significant modification in their services from Gdańsk. The abandonment of the Helsinki route can, at least in part, be blamed upon Stena's activities, whilst the redirection of services to Nynäshamn and Oxelösund was a direct consequence. Lion presents a direct threat to PZB in the east and now operates a ferry that is of superior quality. PZB's reaction to this is one that is common in Poland at the moment in the state sector - surprise and resentment that such competition should be allowed and a tactical failure to respond adequately (at least partly because of lack of resources). This latter failing may quickly change with privatisation. PZB even go so far to suggest that the state should intervene once again to "plan" ferry provision and co-ordinate operations in the east to ensure that competitors from outside Poland do not grow too strong or too quickly. This contrasts significantly with the trend in Poland generally towards a new liberalised market environment.

PZB thus face threats from outside Poland, competition on traditional marketplaces from inside Poland and a difficult privatisation environment. This leads us to their most dramatic response to all this - "Boomerang". "Boomerang" represents a very sizeable investment for PZB - the biggest ever made - into a market that they claim is overtonnaged and thus one that is likely to be unprofitable. PZB's reasons for "Boomerang" stem from a need to be seen to be modernising and developing, coupled with a desire to be more attractive for privatisation and to compete directly in terms of image with Unity Line and the "Polonia". One wonders whether these reasons are adequate for such a step and that the moves taken by the company to reduce manning/employees and to prepare internally for privatisation, although less public, are in fact more significant.

Conclusions

PZB presents a fascinating example of the old and new maritime Poland. Its future is far from secure and it could well be that its new owners, whoever they are, will remove the "Polferries" name from the marketplace, sell off most of the vessels, reduce operations and thus rationalise the market itself. The story of the company and how it finds itself in its current position is a function of old resentments and arguments and this has encouraged PZB both to react with new vessels and the renewal of others, and the creation of new routes, and to demand protection from the centre. The latter is unlikely to be forthcoming and with the growing strength (if only political so far, but likely to be increasingly financial) of PZM and Polish Ocean Lines it would appear likely that PZB may have to succumb to their ownership ambitions. That will depend, at least in part, upon the alternative buyers in the privatisation process that will emerge in 1997/1998 and the opportunities that they provide for the company. It is the Ministry that will decide upon the successful bidder and, thus, it is they who will determine the fate of PZB as a whole. The conclusion of this process is not expected until well into 1998 and even then may not be entirely clear-cut for some time to follow. As such it represents one of the most interesting of all the developments taking place within the Polish maritime sector and one that provides excellent examples of many of the trends and difficulties that are faced by the ex-state organisations as they attempt to adapt to the market and the competitive environment that exists, emerging not only from those entering the marketplace from outside of Poland, but also from the industry as it was before the liberalisation phase of the late 1980s and early 1990s and from the new private sector now developing. PZB's future is one to keep watching as the new maritime Poland continues to adjust, develop and progress from the state controlled sector of the past.

Polska Żegluga Morska
(Polish Steamship Company)

Introduction

Polska Żegluga Morska (PZM), commonly known also as the Polish Steamship Company, has always been a dominantly bulk shipping company which has grown and developed on the back of the Polish coal industry - one of the biggest in the world - but which has actively diversified into other bulk trades and also into operations elsewhere in the world. It is currently the biggest Polish shipping company and the largest tramping ship company in Europe. It regularly transports 27m tonnes of cargo a year and has an annual turnover of US$350m. Recent years have also seen moves into the ferry trades as we shall see in a later section. PZM is probably the most famous of the three Polish ship operators that has emerged from the state run system, and certainly has been, and continues to be the biggest, even though it has now been restructured into a series of smaller operators. Its recent history has revealed all the trends that are apparent throughout the redevelopment of the Polish maritime sector and its place within the industry is not without contention and dispute. In this chapter we shall concentrate in particular upon the changing role that the parent company now performs, the relationships it has with the other two ship operating companies and the prospects for success in the coming years.

A brief history

PZM has always been and continues to be based in Szczecin in the far north west of Poland and close to the German border. Its activities commenced as a state owned ship operator under the new Communist government on the 2nd January 1951 based upon the ownership of initially eight (24000 DWT), soon expanded to 11 small vessels of 27000 DWT trading, mainly operating in the Baltic and the North Sea but with some short distance (coastal and inland) tramping. By 1968, PZM had grown substantially to outstrip all other Polish operators - Polish Ocean Lines in particular - both in terms of ships operated and their tonnage. At the same time, the fleet expanded into new areas of operation and in particular a number of crude oil tankers were put into service ranging from 135000 to 145000 DWT with the aim of both serving the Polish domestic economy and becoming involved in what was then seen as a lucrative cross trading activity. However, market deterioration soon led to their sale and a withdrawal from these activities, as yet never to return.

PZM's heyday was around 1980 when the fleet numbered 126 vessels, with an average age of seven years and carried some 33m tonnes of cargo - by far the largest proportion being Polish foreign trade. Cross trading, however, did not grow in importance in the way anticipated so that by the mid 1980s some 90% of cargoes by volume were still for Polish international movements. The social unrest of the early 1980s and in particular the imposition of martial law, had a notable impact upon the industrial development and activity within Poland affecting the years 1981 to 1985 most severely and these effects were exacerbated by a continuing depression generally in world freight markets. PZM was affected severely by these problems and thus entered the late 1980s in poor condition. The choice facing the company was clear - either bankruptcy or adapt - and the latter choice was taken with PZM concentrating more and more upon international and crosstrade cargoes and entering into long term agreements with overseas grain houses including Cargill International Geneva, A.C. Toepfer Hamburg and Louis Dreyfus of Paris. By the early 1990s the balance of cargoes had moved to 90% in favour of non-Polish commodities with the benefits of access to increased cargo shares, flexibility in evening out trade inconsistencies over time and of course, opportunities to earn large quantities of hard currency.

Between 1991 and 1994, PZM suffered intensely from the decline in the Polish economy and more importantly, the withdrawal of state support including both cash and indirect protectionism. Salary and second-hand ship import taxation rose substantially, made worse by the imposition of national insurance contributions and 40% purchase tax and 22% VAT which was payable only by Polish registered vessels - deemed to be part of the territory of Poland and thus included within the domestic tax regime. Foreign flag vessels were (and still are) exempt. In the mid 1990s, PZM reacted to this poor financial situation by beginning to flag out and even established the 'Baltic Shipping Corporation', a Netherlands Antilles joint venture which was responsible for manning and mortgages on nine vessels. More of this later.

It will have been noted that PZM had not been privatised and thus has reached the late 1990s still in the hands of the state. However, major company restructuring has taken place as a preliminary to the privatisation process that will (inevitably) follow one day. We shall examine the company structure in the following section.

Company structure

The traumas of the 1990s have forced PZM into a new structural format that focuses upon the original PZM company as a new parent company which has interests in a series of subsidiaries that have responsibility in turn for the operations of the group. PZM is left with responsibility for management, administration and strategy. Most of the new subsidiaries are dependent private companies (in the Polish sense of the term) subject to Polish Commercial law, whilst PZM itself remains state owned as a nationalised enterprise. The restructuring process dates back to 28th May 1982 when Żegluga Polska S.A. (ZPSA) of Szczecin (otherwise occasionally known as the Polish Shipping Joint Stock Company) was set up as a wholly owned subsidiary of PZM with 99 vessels purchased from its owner. The creation of ZPSA was undertaken because of a threat to PZM vessels of arrest and sale from foreign creditors due to default on mortgage payments by PZM. Placing the vessels under ZPSA's ownership divorced them from PZM and the latter's debts thus securing the vessels within PZM's control and yet safe from creditors. ZPSA continued to act as a vessel holding company until 1993 when it began to take on the role of actual operator as well. It remains 100% owned by PZM to this day and retains ownership of a large number of the company's vessels.

In addition to the actions taken with respect to ZPSA and in response to dire financial problems, PZM's activities in the market place have also been allocated to some 36 subsidiary companies who are located largely in the private sector and who have independence from PZM as a holding company and yet are partially owned by the latter. These subsidiaries are listed in Figure 19. They represent all the activities of the parent company that were undertaken up to the point of restructuring, but in a way similar to the process at Polish Ocean Lines, these activities have been split up into new operating companies with responsibility for success and with clearly and closely defined profit and loss centres. This concentrates experience, knowledge and attitudes to work and helps to focus attention upon the market place. Location in the Polish private sector also ensures that all the benefits of the Commercial Law are realised including freedom from union interference in management decisions and the possibility of employee involvement in profits. There are no Workers Councils to consider and decision-making is easier, faster and more directed towards the immediate problem in hand.

Subsidiary activity and creation is also linked in the need to move some activities overseas to realise full financial benefits and to avoid domestic taxation and also to the diversification of the company's operations and interests as PZM has begun to get involved in the ferry sector, ships supplies, ship finance, property development and land deals.

Management of the parent company rests through a Board, consisting of a General Director assisted by a Finance Director, Economic Policy Director, Technical and Investment Director and Human Resources and Administration Director. In addition, although they are not Board Members, are an Assistant General Director and Marketing Department Manager. The Board reports directly to their owners, formerly the Ministry of Maritime Economy but from 1996 the State Treasury. Many of these Board members and those of the subsidiaries also sit on other subsidiary boards, thus making the whole organisation highly co-ordinated and structured, but also very complex. There is no doubt that the subsidiaries are independent in their operations and decision-making, but at the same time, similar to Polish Ocean Lines, there remains a lingering doubt about the degree of complexity and the inter-relationships that must exist between parent and children.

The functions of the extensive series of companies in which PZM has interests are not always clear and we cannot attempt to analyse this complex web of interests in full here. They represent a number of decisions by PZM - to become more diversified; to protect financial interests; to facilitate access to financial markets; to remove PZM from a series of earlier collaborative ventures including PSAL Antwerp, Gdynia America London and Gdynia America New York which included Polish Ocean Lines in their make-up, thus increasing levels of independence. Some indication of the more interesting relationships and activities can be pointed out.

PZM itself is now only a holding company with responsibility for all or parts of the companies beneath it. It still owns some ships (see Figure 20) but relatively few. It exists as the state interest in this shipping sector and although due for privatisation, this is likely to be delayed for an indeterminate period of time. As a state company, PZM remains restricted by the operation of Workers Councils, the activities of trades unions, controls on pay and issues related to social fund payments. Moves towards privatisation are slowly being made but have suffered a stop/start process for political reasons.

Figure 19
PZM subsidiary companies, 1997.

Company	Owner(s) (%)
PZM	State(100)
ZPSA SA	PZM (100)
Polsteam Luxembourg SA	ZPSA (100)
PAZIM JV Ltd	PZM (100)
Polsteam Oceantramp Ltd	PZM (19), ZPSA (30), Others (51)
Polsteam Shortramp Ltd	PZM (19), ZPSA (30), Others (51)
Polsteam Tankers Ltd	PZM (19), ZPSA (30), Others (51)
Polsteam Brokers Ltd	ZPSA (40.83), Others (59.17)
Polsteam Supply SA	ZPSA (30), Polsteam Lux. (4), Others (66)
Polsteam Consulting Ltd	ZPSA (37.5), Others (62.5)
Polonia Line Ltd	ZPSA (50), Others (50)
Unity Line Ltd	ZPSA (50), Others (50)
Baltic Atlantic Shg Co. I	PZM (100)
Baltic Atlantic Shg Co. II	PZM (66), Others (34)
Polsteam Ag. de Nav Ltda	PZM (100)
Polascamar S.r.l.	PZM (54), Others (46)
Polhansa Shipping GmbH	PZM (40), Others(60)
Polbaltica A/B	PZM (40), Others (60)
Polsteam USA Inc.	ZPSA (100)
Diamond Bay Enterprises	ZPSA (100)
Steamlib Ltd	ZPSA (100)
Steampol Ltd	ZPSA (100)
Polsteam UK Ltd	Polsteam Lux. (100)
Polsteam Benelux BV	Polsteam Lux. (100)
Polsteam Iberia SA	Polsteam Lux. (100)
Fairlakes Ltd.	Polsteam Lux. (100)
Daria Shipping Ltd.	Polsteam Lux. (100)
Polclip Luxembourg SA	Polsteam Lux. (50), Others (50)
EuroAfrica Shipping Lines	PZM (28), Others (72)

NB "Others" includes in the majority of cases, a substantial proportion owned by employees.

Source :- PZM, 1996

Full privatisation is not expected before 1999 at the earliest and so the restructuring that has taken place through the subsidiary companies remains the main way forward at the moment. **ZPSA**, as we noted earlier, is the group's biggest ship-owner and acts as a legal buffer between PZM and the financial problems that the latter company had in the 1980s and the time of martial law and continues to face although these have lessened from the most difficult times of the early 1990s. **Polsteam Luxembourg SA** is based in Luxembourg and provides access to financial resources outside of Poland and a further level of financial protection. It also represents PZM and its subsidiaries in that part of Europe and is responsible for organising the movement of large and complex quantities of money outside Poland between the various overseas PZM Group companies that now exist.

PAZIM Ltd is a product of the joint venture established between PZM and an Austrian builder for the development and construction of the sizeable, 24 storey PAZIM hotel and business centre in Szczecin which has been open since December 1992 and with the hotel sector operationally managed by the international hotel group Radisson. Continuously troubled by financial difficulties, and with a large debt overhang that continues to be problematic, the Austrian part of the joint venture, constructor Ilbau, withdrew in early 1997 leading to a debt refinancing and the development is now owned entirely by PZM, who thus are responsible for the debt, and managed overall by PAZIM Ltd. PZM and many of its subsidiaries are based there although the financial arrangements for renting the property from PAZIM are unclear. Detail from PZM in September 1997 reaffirmed the continued problems with the development with the financing of the site still the greatest drain on PZM's budget. Utilisation had improved greatly with the shopping and services space 100% taken and the office space 85%; the hotel had a utilisation ratio of between 47 and 50%.

Polsteam Oceantramp Ltd is a subsidiary of PZM set up on the 1st July 1993 and owned jointly with ZPSA, that was established to operate deep sea international bulk shipping activities and emerged from the old PZM following the reconstruction of the company in the 1990s with 56 vessels. Dominant cargoes are those of coal, grain, phosphorites and iron ore, although other commodities are not insignificant. Polsteam Oceantramp is the largest of the PZM operators (responsible for vessels between 23000 and 74000 DWT) although it owns no ships itself. The predominant owner is ZPSA although some remain with PZM and a few are owned overseas for financial reasons.

Polsteam Shortramp Ltd is also a subsidiary of PZM and set up on the same day and in identical fashion to Polsteam Oceantramp, but concentrates upon the short sea bulk market place where it offers full operational short sea shipping services, as well as associated agency and chartering facilities. It operates 43 bulk carrier vessels in the range 4400 to 16700 DWT owned by a large number of independent off shore companies to facilitate financial procedures, but also a number remain with ZPSA. The company employs 65 staff and also provides a full agency service for all PZM vessels calling at Szczecin, Świnoujście and Police.

Polsteam Tankers Ltd we will discuss in a later chapter but for completeness here, we can record that they are tanker specialists who at present (1997) concentrate upon the liquid sulphur market, but who are considering further expansion into the oils sector. They emerged, along with and on the same day as Polsteam Oceantramp and Polsteam Shortramp, from the original PZM structure and own no vessels of their own, ZPSA is the dominant partner here. The exception is the new "Penelope", owned by a Liberian based company, thus facilitating its finance.

Polsteam Brokers Ltd is an in-house broking team, with additional interests in chartering and forwarding, that was set up within PZM in September 1992 following the liberalisation phases of the early 1990s and in response to a recognition of the amount of broking work that the company was farming out to independent brokers. It was hoped that this internal work could be allied to broking activities for other shipping companies in Poland, and Polsteam Brokers has managed to establish itself as a major competitor to Polfracht and other broking firms. The company employs seven brokers in Szczecin and five more in its branch office in Gdynia. **Polsteam Supply**, was established in a similar way to provide technical and deck supplies for ships anywhere in the world including safety and engine room equipment both from the PZM group and others from Poland and overseas using their experience and market position gathered over the years. They possess their own forwarding service, heavy trucks and bonded warehouse. Around 150 vessels are under regular contract and some 30000 items are kept in stock at any time. **Polsteam Consulting** is a specialist branch of the PZM Group which provides consultancy advice and chartering and agency mediation for anyone in the maritime sector utilising the skills and data of the PZM Group.

Polonia Line was set up specifically to manage the "Polonia" vessel of Unity Line and is owned jointly (50/50) with EuroAfrica. It is responsible for the management and operation of the vessel. Its activities are closely co-ordinated with those of **Unity Line**, who have responsibility for the ferry activities of that business including their marketing and other related duties. Unity Line is again owned 50/50 with EuroAfrica. Meanwhile some 28% of **EuroAfrica** itself was acquired in December 1997 from Polish Ocean Lines, Bel Leasing Co. and Bank Inicjatyw Gospodarzcych. This acquisition represents one of the earliest moves in the formation of a single ex-state owned shipping company between the two major players - PZM and Polish Ocean Lines.

Polsteam Agencia de Navegacao Ltda is the subsidiary company of PZM based in Brazil in Rio de Janeiro and represent the interests of the group in South America generally. Similar companies exist in the Netherlands

(**Polsteam Benelux B.V.**), the USA (**Polsteam USA Inc.**), Italy (**Polascamar S.r.l.**), Sweden (**Polbaltica A/B**), Spain (**Polsteam Iberia S.A.**), the United Kingdom (**Polsteam UK Ltd**) and Germany (**Polhansa Shipping GmbH**) with varying ownership patterns between 100% to 0% PZM, 100% ZPSA and 100% Polsteam Luxembourg.

Steamlib Ltd and **Steampol Ltd** are both ship-owning companies 100% owned themselves by ZPSA and who have responsibilities for "Batalion Czwartakow" and "Zaglebie Miedziowe" respectively - both vessels operating within the Polsteam Oceantramp organisation. The former company and vessel are registered in Liberia, whilst the latter are in the Marshall Islands. Other companies in this ship-owning category include **Daria Shipping**, the owner of "Daria", another Polsteam Oceantramp vessel.

This company group structure suggests two trends - the first relates to the desire of PZM to diversify their interests (e.g. into ship supply, ferry operations, broking and consultancy) with the obvious benefits of financial security and the reduction in market stress and secondly an additional, if not more significant objective, in protecting the group's assets and opening pathways to additional and cheaper finance for ship operation and purchase (including the various new ship owning companies, and those located in the USA and Luxembourg). Two results of this process are flagging out - which is slowly occurring across the fleet and has resulted in the movement of vessels to the Marshall Islands, Vanuatu and Cyprus - and complexity; it is now increasingly difficult to disentangle responsibility and ownership through the group as new companies are created with board members commonly shared.

The PZM Group is also represented by a number of agents overseas including offices in Tunisia, France and Morocco.

Vessels

The range of vessels that are operated by the PZM Group is indicated in Figure 20 divided between the four operators of Polsteam Oceantramp, Polsteam Shortramp, Polsteam Tankers and the joint venture with EuroAfrica, Unity Line. The majority remain under the Polish flag but an increasing number, and particularly new vessels (for example "Penelope" of Polsteam Tankers, and "Polonia" of Unity Line) , are located elsewhere with flags of convenience. A large number of Polsteam Shortramp ships have been placed with the Marshall Islands flag particularly those of a smaller size. Other flags used include Cyprus, Bahamas and Vanuatu. The new vessels are always flagged outside Poland even if ordered from a Polish yard (commonly a political necessity even today), as if they are flagged domestically they are treated as a domestic order and are subject to 22% value added tax, plus a number of other charges. If ordered by a company from abroad - even if it is effectively owned by PZM - it becomes an export order and thus is exempt taxation. Orders from outside Poland, but for domestic companies, are treated as imports and subject to heavy taxation up to 40%. Discussions on this issue continue with the state. By late 1997, around 40% of all PZM vessels were with flags of convenience saving an estimated 100000-200000US$ per vessel per year in Polish national insurance contributions.

The oldest vessel dates from 1970, and there are a substantial number from the 1970s and early 1980s still operating regularly. Newer vessels tend to be bigger, thus replacing a larger number of smaller vessels and thus reducing the fleet in size, a process that is likely to continue.

Ownership is very varied, spread between PZM, the original owners of all the vessels, through ZPSA as a buffer owner, to individual ship owning companies located overseas, helping to facilitate access to cheaper finance and other flags. The PZM owned vessels are commonly the older vessels and are also commonly Polish flagged. These ships also commonly have no debt attached to them although they retain some residual value and hence can be used as collateral for borrowing money for shipping activities elsewhere.

Total fleet size of the Group in mid 1997 was 129 vessels of 3.5m DWT and with a market value estimated at almost US$ 1 billion and an average age of around 15.5 years.

Figure 20
PZM. Fleet 1997

Polsteam Oceantramp

Vessel	Flag	Built	DWT	Owner
Armia Krajowa	POL	1991	73505	DIFKO
Legiony Polskie	POL	1991	73505	DIFKO
Orlęta Lwowskie	POL	1991	73505	DIFKO
Szare Szeregi	POL	1991	73505	DIFKO
Polska Walcząca	POL	1992	73505	DIFKO
Solidarność	POL	1991	73470	DIFKO
Bełchatów	POL	1976	71277	PZM
Huta Katowice	POL	1976	64484	ZPSA
Huta Sendzimira	POL	1976	64337	ZPSA
Ossolineum	POL	1985	61013	PZM
Manifest PKWN	POL	1986	60969	PZM
Uniwersytet Gdański	POL	1974	52020	ZPSA
Uniwersytet Warszawski	POL	1974	52020	ZPSA

Figure 20 continued

Vessel	Flag	Built	DWT	Owner
Uniwersytet Wrocławski	POL	1974	52020	ZPSA
Uniwersytet Jagielloński	POL	1971	52000	ZPSA
Diana	CYP	1997	41260	Diana Sh.
Daria	CYP	1995	41260	Daria Shg
Cerinthius	BHS	1988	40009	Hadley S.
Generał Grot-Rowecki	POL	1985	38498	ZPSA
Generał Berling	POL	1984	38466	ZPSA
Generał Pradzyński	POL	1976	37873	ZPSA
Generał Bem	POL	1974	37844	ZPSA
Generał Jasiński	POL	1974	37844	ZPSA
Generał Madaliński	POL	1975	37844	ZPSA
Powstaniec Styczniowy	POL	1986	33780	ZPSA
Powstaniec Listopadowy	POL	1985	33767	ZPSA
Batalion Czwartaków	LBR	1986	33767	ZPSA
Maciej Rataj	POL	1985	33750	ZPSA
Rodło	POL	1985	33742	ZPSA
Major Hubal	POL	1985	33725	ZPSA
Armia Ludowa	POL	1987	33640	ZPSA
Ignacy Daszyński	POL	1988	33639	ZPSA
Stanislaw Kulczyński	POL	1988	33627	ZPSA
Bataliony Chłopskie	POL	1988	33618	ZPSA
Oksywie	POL	1987	33580	ZPSA
Reduta Ordona	POL	1978	33490	ZPSA
Walka Młodych	POL	1978	33485	ZPSA
Uniwerytet Śląski	POL	1979	33470	ZPSA
Mirosławiec	POL	1975	33450	ZPSA
Powstaniec Wielkopolski	POL	1974	33450	ZPSA
Studzianki	POL	1974	33450	ZPSA
Tobruk II	POL	1972	33377	ZPSA
Obrońcy Poczty	POL	1971	32196	ZPSA
Powstaniec Śląski	POL	1970	32193	ZPSA
Narwik II	POL	1972	31922	ZPSA
Cedynia	POL	1973	31910	ZPSA
Syn Pułku	POL	1974	31910	ZPSA
Pomorze Zachodnie	POL	1984	26696	PZM
Ziemia Gnieźnieńska	POL	1984	26696	PZM
Ziema Tarnowska	POL	1985	26678	PZM
Ziema Chelmińska	POL	1984	26642	PZM

Figure 20 continued

Vessel	Flag	Built	DWT	Owner
Ziemia Suwalska	POL	1984	26605	PZM
Ziemia Zamojska	POL	1984	26605	PZM
Ziemia Krakowska	POL	1971	23792	ZPSA
Zaglebie Miedziowe	MHL	1971	23790	Steampol
Ziemia Lubelska	POL	1971	23785	ZPSA
Ziemia Bialostocka	POL	1972	23736	ZPSA
Ziemia Olsztyńska	POL	1973	23719	ZPSA

Polsteam Shortramp

Vessel	Flag	Built	DWT	Owner
Clipper Eagle	BHS	1994	16906	Clipper Eagle
Clipper Falcon	BHS	1994	16900	Clipper Eagle
Fossnes	NIS	1995	16890	Rega Shg
Fjordnes	NIS	1995	16880	Drawa Sg
Jamno	MHL	1979	16813	Jamno I
Gardno	MHL	1980	16753	Gardno I
Tałty	MHL	1979	16728	Talty Inc
Wadag	MHL	1980	16753	Wadag I
Roś	MHL	1979	16653	Ros Inc
Wigry	MHL	1979	16653	Wigry Inc
Mamry	MHL	1979	16653	Mamry
Kopalnia Sosnowiec	POL	1974	14179	ZPSA
Huta Zgoda	POL	1974	14179	ZPSA
Kopalnia Wałbrzych	POL	1975	14176	ZPSA
Kopalnia Zofliówka	POL	1975	14176	ZPSA
Rolnik	POL	1975	14176	ZPSA
Budowlany	POL	1976	14164	ZPSA
Huta Zygmunt	POL	1976	14164	ZPSA
Kopalnia Machów	POL	1972	14065	ZPSA
Wislanes	VUT	1992	13770	Wisla Sg
Odranes	BHS	1992	13759	Odra Shg
Nidanes	BHS	1992	13759	Nida Shg
Wartanes	BHS	1993	13759	Warta Sg
Kopalnia Piaseczno	POL	1971	13716	ZPSA
Kopalnia Jeziórko	POL	1971	13665	ZPSA
Kopalnia Szczyglowice	POL	1969	12480	ZPSA

Figure 20 continued

Vessel	Flag	Built	DWT	Owner
Kopalnia Borynia	POL	1989	11898	PZM
Kopalnia Ziemovit	POL	1989	11772	ZPSA
Kopalnia Halemba	POL	1990	11715	PZM
Kopalnia Rydułtowy	POL	1990	11702	PZM
Malbork II	MHL	1980	4461	Sitno Shg
Bytom	MHL	1980	4459	Sitno Shg
Łomza	MHL	1980	4459	Kolno Sg
Goleniów	MHL	1980	4459	Sitno Shg
Mielec	MHL	1980	4456	Kolno Sg
Warka	MHL	1980	4451	Sitno Shg
Wieluń	MHL	1980	4447	Kolno Sg
Kościerzyna	MHL	1980	4443	Kolno Sg
Mława	MHL	1979	4415	Kolno Sg
Zgorzeiec	MHL	1980	4412	Sitno Shg
Bolesławiec	MHL	1979	4390	Goplo Sg
Wyszków	MHL	1979	4378	Goplo Sg
Chorzów	MHL	1980	4361	Goplo Sg
Sieradz	MHL	1979	4361	Goplo Sg
Gniezno II	MHL	1979	4358	Goplo Sg

Polsteam Tankers

Vessel	Flag	Built	DWT	Owner
Penelope	BHS	1996	15329	Ina Shg
Tarnobrzeg II	POL	1974	9814	ZPSA
Zaglębie Siarkowe	POL	1976	9783	ZPSA
Siarkopol	POL	1974	9750	ZPSA
Prof K. Bohdanowicz	POL	1974	9694	ZPSA

Unity Line

Vessel	Flag	Built	DWT	Owner
Polonia	BHS	1995	1000 pass	Unity L
Jan Śniadecki	POL	1979	14417 GRT	Unity L
Mikołaj Kopernik	POL	1979	8734 GRT	Unity L

Flags :- POL = Poland; BHS = Bahamas; MHL = Marshall Islands; VUT = Vanuatu; CYP = Cyprus; LBR = Liberia.

Source : PZM, 1997

Recent commercial activity and employment

Apart from relatively small interests in the ferry sector, the PZM Group is essentially a bulk cargo operation with a sizeable number of ancillary and subsidiary activities that have been spun off from the core over the years since liberalisation of the Polish economy. Despite the poor years of the late 1980s and early 1990s, the Group has shown growth during the mid 1990s so that cargo carried has stabilised and even, to a limited extent, increased since 1992 (see Figure 21).

These figures place the PZM Group as the biggest tramping organisation in Europe. Growth has been achieved through improvements in the Group's structure and organisation resulting in a marked reduction in the number of voyages in ballast, an improvement in dead-weight utilisation, a reduction in voyage cycles and a marked improvement in employment productivity. All these effects have occurred as an indirect consequence of the liberalisation of the Polish maritime market.

Figure 21
PZM Group vessel cargo

	Value mUS$	Volume (million tons)
1990	350	23.8
1991	355	23.4
1992	318	23.1
1993	320	25.0
1994	330	26.2
1995	384	26.4

Source :-PZM, 1996

Within this growth, crosstrading has dominated increasingly and although the Polish economy is now recovering quickly, it remains the area of future growth activity. June 1997 estimates of crosstrading activities within the group placed them as representing some 93.3% of all shipments, with Polish based trade accounting for the other 6.7%. This is a dramatic shift from the mid 1980s when the respective figures were 40% crosstrade and 60% domestic, with the major changes in proportions occurring between 1988 and 1990, by which time the level of crosstrading had grown to around 70%.

Recent figures also show that the cargoes carried by PZM Group owned vessels are dominated by grain (rising from 4.0m tonnes in the first half of 1996, to 4.6m tonnes in the first half of 1997) and phosporites (although a decline was evident here during the same period, from 4.0m tonnes to 3.8m tonnes), with coal (rising from 1.9m to 2.1m tonnes) close behind. Iron ore was also important, although falling from 1.9 to 1.3m tonnes, and liquid cargo represented another decline from 231000 to 219000 tonnes. Many of the vessels are also on time charter. These commodities have always been important to the Group even before the late 1980s, but under the old regime, time chartering was rare and coal held the dominant position. The change in commodities reflects the changing economy of Poland and the moves towards crosstrade markets.

The small ferry interests of the group, through their joint ownership of Unity Line with EuroAfrica, appeared to have improved figures between the first half of 1996 and that of 1997. Trucks and trailers increased from 26662 to 24308; coaches from 387 to 271; cars from 15593 to 17283 and passengers from 67611 to 68130. However, despite the rise in loadings, overall utilisation, particularly on the passenger/car/leisure sector remained poor. More of this can be found in the earlier chapter on Polska Żegluga Bałtycka.

Employment structures have also changed substantially since the mid 1980s with a static volume of DWT under the Group's control but a steady reduction in both shore based and sea going staff, particularly in the latter. Far fewer employees are now engaged directly by PZM and increasing numbers are working aboard foreign flag vessels (by 1997 nearly 30% of the Group's employees). Onshore personnel represented around 10% and crews on Polish vessels around 60%. This trend away from Polish vessel crews will, naturally, decline as the fleet moves into other flags and as new vessels are acquired also flagged away from Poland. By late 1997, PZM employed around 3807 people, including 3238 seafarers on ships with Polish flags and 569 staff ashore. On foreign flagged vessels, not all PZM owned, there were another 1630 seafarers.

Vessel renewal and replacement

Fleet renewal presents continuing problems for PZM as the financial constraints remain severe and it is impossible to sustain a fleet renewal programme that is adequate for the fleet size that exists at the moment. The trend towards flagging out and the continued transfer of vessels to overseas based companies is a direct response to the financial difficulties faced by the PZM Group in this area and will undoubtedly continue. No new acquisitions will be Polish flagged.

Under the restructured Group, the first newbuildings were ordered in 1995 and included two 'Handysize' vessels from Varna shipyard in Bulgaria, each of 41450 DWT for delivery in 1997, plus five vessels from the Szczecin shipyard to be built between 1998 and 2000. These latter included two 15500

DWT liquid sulphur tankers for Polsteam Tankers and three 16900 DWT bulk carriers which are a continuation of an order delivered to the PZM Group between 1994 and 1995. One of these became the "Penelope", which was converted for the liquid sulphur market and transferred to Polsteam Tankers.

Further details of PZM's strategy for fleet renewal emerged during September and October of 1997 with a general statement that 24-36 vessels would be purchased and firm plans to order five 'Panamax' bulkers and five lake-sized vessels of around 34600 DWT as part of a 15 vessel renewal programme costing a total of US$800m. This was part of the continuing process within the company of lowering the average age of the fleet which had reached almost 16 years by late 1997. Both sales and purchases were planned to increase from a very low level of only two sales and one purchase in 1996 - low given the fleet size of over 100 vessels. Five more vessels were due to be sold during 1997, all over 23 years of age, whilst two newbuildings were expected to enter service including a bulker from Varna shipyard and another from an Indonesian shipyard originally destined for a United Kingdom owner.

Further fleet development plans included the adaptation of "Fjordnes", a bulker on time charter, to a liquid sulphur tanker for Polsteam Tankers of Gdynia following the path of the "Penelope" and on order in late 1997 were two further liquid sulphur carriers of 15500 DWT each and three bulkers of 16900 DWT.

The construction of the five 'lakers' was expected to be straightforward and undertaken through a US$100m contract by Mitsui Engineering and Shipbuilding at the Japanese shipyard at Chiba near Tokyo, a decision heavily influenced by a financial package involving preferential Japanese government credit facilities and also a history of PZM co-operation with Japanese shipbuilding that dates back to 1975 (42). The vessels, which are expected to be flagged with Cyprus, are destined for trade between Europe and the Great Lakes and thus are designed to a narrow breadth. However, the five 'Panamax' sized bulkers had quickly become embroiled in a political argument stemming from the imminent financial collapse of the Gdańsk shipyard, and a desire amongst some political quarters for orders to be directed towards the yard. PZM and the yard seemingly failed to reach agreement, although the final outcome of the negotiations was far from clear (6,52,64,73,74).

All recent plans for renewals have been financed by internal sources - up to 20% of the cost - and in a new move in both the Polish shipping and banking markets, by domestic banking institutions from late 1997.

Profits and turnover

The large majority of revenue in the group is realised through mainstream commercial freight activity and is dominated by PZM cargo shipping work. Other activities included chartering out of vessels, and passenger and agency services. PZM reported a turnover of some US $339m in 1994, rising to US $384m in 1995 and with a projected turnover of between US $340-355m for 1996. Profit/loss figures were not readily available but were expected to be around break-even in 1996 despite a drop of around 60% in rates for that year over 1995. Profit for 1995 was about US $26m, benefiting from a 23% rate rise that year following a variously quoted break-even or small loss position in 1994. Particularly notable was the fact that the PAZIM hotel and property investment costs were at last being controlled by 1995 with claims that the hotel itself contributed some US $1m to 1995 profits. Later figures are not available and even this latter figure appears a little doubtful considering the size of the debt that the development represents.

The future - a discussion

The PZM Group has many ideas for the future, but in tune with the break up of the Group into individual companies with some level of independent action and decision-making, these plans are increasingly becoming separate ones with a reduction in the interdependence and co-ordination that exists between them.

One plan that in 1997 came to nothing was a central government sponsored proposal that PZM should be part of a consortium to purchase and revive the ailing shipbuilding industry of Poland and more specifically the Szczecin shipyard in conjunction with a Polish marine engine builder and bankers. Meanwhile, the five year investment plan adopted by PZM in 1996 provides a general direction for ship replacement and renewal into the twenty-first century. The main areas of investment are intended to be 'Lakemax', 'Panamax' and 'Handysize' tonnage, as evidenced by the recent orders that were discussed above. Both a minimum and a maximum order plan has been agreed; the minimum envisages newbuildings totalling 940000 DWT (26 vessels) and the maximum 1310000 DWT (34 vessels). Second-hand purchases are not excluded but will be determined by the state of the market both for cargo and vessels.

PZM presents a large number of issues that are dominant within the Polish maritime sector and which in many ways, typify the progress of the former state monoliths in the shipping sector as they attempt to adapt to the new environment within the economy. We can mention only a few of these issues here but hope that the reader will recognise many others that are apparent from the details and discussion given above.

In terms of new vessels and the replacement of older ones, PZM is now proceeding with a slow but steady reduction in fleet size accompanied by the indirect benefits of a lowering average fleet age. Finance of these new vessels is universally now through overseas companies, utilising foreign flags, although increasingly using Polish banks and financial sources - a significant change in the financial methods used in Poland.

PZM retains the protective framework it has adopted over the years through the establishment of ZPSA and subsequently the series of smaller companies used as owners for individual vessels. Despite PZM's increasingly strong financial position, this arrangement has worked so well that there are no signs that it will be dismantled. This framework is also the cause of the highly complex legal and ownership position that now surrounds PZM and which gives it an aura of modernity but also subterfuge. The privatisation process will do nothing to reduce this situation - although relatively little seems to be happening on this front by late 1997. This is at least in part, a function of the financial problems of PZM but also the lack of desire within the company to move from what might be seen as a comfortably protected position at the moment. The sheer complexity of the process must also hinder developments of this sort.

PZM's problems financially have stemmed from a combination of events largely beyond their control - i.e. the impact of social and economic change on the Polish economy - and others that are largely self-imposed including the disastrous investment in property in Szczecin. This latter problem has a considerable overhang but is at last retreating as a major issue. Lessons for many other state company investors have been learned from the experience of PZM in this sector and few, if any, other investments of this sort are likely to follow in the foreseeable future.

PZM's continued squabble with PZB and the recent moves towards acquiring a stake in the soon to be (late 1997) privatised ferry and coastal shipping company also reflects a continuing trend within the Polish maritime sector, as a legacy from the old state dominated days, and more significantly in this case, a continuing argument fuelled by resentment over the issues stemming from the establishment of PZB from PZM and Polish Ocean Lines and the more recent Unity Lines farce. The purchase of "Polonia", and the "Boomerang" effect are all examples of the poor relations that exist between the two companies and the worsening of this situation as the western Baltic marketplace becomes heavily overtonnaged as a result of the failure to co-ordinate services and the determination of both operators to outdo the other. PZM are likely to be the winners in all this if only because of their sheer size and thus, political and economic influence, and they may well be successful in purchasing, with POL, a large stake of PZB. But in time the only true winners are likely to be ferry operators from elsewhere - e.g. Stena Line - as the Polish operators destroy their own market dominance in the process of concluding their arguments.

There are many other issues that could be discussed here, but those outlined above give a good taste of the problems within the industry and within the Group as a whole. Privatisation will eventually emerge as a force, and in the meantime the restructuring process will continue with the formation of 'private' companies (at least under Polish Commercial Law) each operating in an individual, yet co-ordinated fashion, and each largely owned by PZM itself or interests of the company. This situation is very reminiscent of the situation that also holds at Polish Ocean Lines and which is also likely to run on for some time. The restructured format does at least have the benefit of focusing ideas and upon markets and, as such, can only benefit the group as it attempts to continue to adapt to the new environment.

Port Gdynia

Introduction

Morski Port Handłowy Gdynia S.A. - or more commonly known as Port Gdynia - is one of the three major international port authorities in Poland which until the early 1990s were the only permitted port entry/exit points into and out of the country and which remain predominant in market share compared with the minor developments that have occurred in any other locations on the Baltic Coast. Other sections deal with the other two competitors in Gdańsk and Szczecin/Świnoujście whilst here we will concentrate upon developments in Gdynia.

Whilst this text concentrates upon the changes occurring in Polish shipping, it would be unrealistic and not too helpful to leave out from this discussion the developments in the ports sector - hence their inclusion - which provide an essential organisational and infrastructural element in the shipping logistical network. In particular, this section will focus upon the activities of the port today, the development of the port to its current position, the recent major organisational changes that have affected Polish ports in recent years, and finally the prospects for the future and in particular the impact upon the ship operators of changing operational, managerial and organisational practices. Some briefly summarised details of trends in the port's activities are given in Figure 22 for the years 1990 to 1995. Figures for 1997 show a sizeable increase in volumes on 1996 (some 17% for the first six months), which in turn had shown an improvement of 12.1% on 1995. These 1997 increases included a dramatic rise in oil imports and also sizeable improvements in grain handling. Predicted volumes for the year 2010 suggest a rise from around 8.56 million tonnes in 1996 to between 11.76 and 15.72 million tonnes with the strongest growth in general cargo (37, 38, 39, 66).

Port development

Gdynia is very much a modern city as it was developed by the Poles only from 1921 as a response to the theoretical independence of Gdańsk and the practicalities of the latter's domination by German interests. Szczecin (Stettin), at this time was also located within German territory. Thus Gdynia was developed as the only Polish international port located on the 72km of coastal territory allocated to her under the Treaty of Versailles. Work began in 1923 providing facilities firstly, for the Polish navy and subsequently, soon after for commercial ships. By 1934 the initial phase of the port was completed with a handling capacity of 10 million tonnes - both exports of Polish coal and a considerable amount of imports to the country were brought in through Gdynia.

The second world war led to the destruction of the majority of the port infrastructure and immediately after the war, and the return of Gdańsk to Poland, Gdynia found itself with a new competitor. The Port of Gdynia became a focus of industrial unrest against the Communist regime during the 1980s in a similar fashion to the developments in Gdańsk. It now acts as one of the three international ports of Poland, along with Gdańsk and Szczecin/Świnoujście which are having to face the major changes occurring in the Polish economy in general, and Polish shipping in particular. It was reconstituted as a state owned joint stock company in 1991 along with the other two international ports.

Readjustment

Under recent efforts to bring the whole of the Polish ports industry up to date, Gdynia has restructured both the operation and management of the port through the creation of a series of new companies. The ownership of the port authority has also been reconstituted, along with the other international ports, following new legislation introduced in 1997 (72). New owners of the Port Authority are now 51% state Treasury and the remainder split between the local (Gdynia) city authority and private sector port operators, rather than 100% state ownership as was previously the case.

Gdynia Port Authority had already, prior to these most recent changes, introduced four main operating subsidiaries in a bid to reduce the bureaucratic and monolithic hand of the old structure and to streamline operations so that

Figure 22
Turnover. Port of Gdynia S.A. 1990-1995 ('000 tonnes)

	1990	1991	1992	1993	1994	1995	1996	1997
Foreign Trade	9157	7026	6097	7066	7072	6727	n.a.	n.a.
Transit	810	227	182	693	933	906	855	880
Coal	2438	1489	1516	2293	2939	2153	1700	n.a.
Ore	807	208	153	4	0	77	86	n.a.
Other bulk	1165	1069	739	722	868	857	1500	n.a.
Grain	1257	784	670	1347	464	527	1600	n.a.
Timber	1	0	44	16	0	0	n.a.	n.a.
Liquid fuels	636	415	513	121	138	357	n.a.	n.a.
General cargo	3663	3298	2644	3256	3596	3662	3600	n.a.
Containerised	1027	999	901	1051	1141	1326	n.a.	n.a.

Source: Port of Gdynia, 1996

there is more incentive to raise quality and react to market demands and eventually to facilitate privatisation. These four main operating subsidiary companies comprise:

> Baltic Container Terminal (Bałtycki Terminal Kontenerowy Sp. z.o.o.) (BCT)
> Baltic Grain terminal (Bałtycki Terminal Zbożowy Sp. z.o.o.) (BGT)
> Maritime Bulk Terminal (Morski Terminal Masowy Gdynia Sp. z.o.o.) (MTMG)
> Baltic General Cargo Terminal (Bałtycki Terminal Drobnicowy Gdynia Sp. z.o.o.) (BTDG)

A series of ancillary companies have also been formed which provide services to the Port Authority and its subsidiaries. These are:

Port Transport Company (Portowy Zakład Transportu Sp. z.o.o.)

Port Supply Company (Portowy Zakład Zaopatrzenia Sp. z.o.o.)

Port Service Company (Portowy Usług Zeglugowych i Portowych Sp. z.o.o.) (WUZ)

In addition to these companies wholly owned by the Port, a strategic interest has also been taken in a number of other organisations including freight forwarders Mirtrans International Forwarding Sp. z.o.o., Terramar Sp. z.o.o. and Uniport Co. Ltd Gdynia, container feeder shipping line operator Baltic Container Lines Co. Ltd (26), inland box terminal operator Speedcont Sp. z.o.o. and combined transport undertaking Polkombi SA.. A large number of minor shareholdings also exist in a variety of industries and enterprises including banks and shipyards. These shareholdings are invariably very small and it is doubtful whether they fulfil any real purpose or fit in with any strategic ambitions.

The new operating companies

(1) Baltic Container Terminal (BCT)

The Baltic Container Terminal is the biggest terminal in Poland and the surrounding region for container import, export and transhipment. In 1995, some 140000 TEU passed through the 50 hectare site (a 16% rise on 1994), increasing to 156000 TEU in 1996 and anticipated to be 170000 TEU in 1997 utilising the Helskie I quay and ro-ro ramp. It is estimated that at this rate, capacity will be reached by 1998 and hence there is a fairly urgent need for expansion - a difficult task as the container terminal is actually located within the city area. It is from the also from this terminal that Lion Ferry operates to and from Karlskrona in Sweden, six times a week - part of the Stena Shipping empire. 1995 saw a passenger throughput of over 90000.

BCT is essentially a feeder port with, for example, some 35000 TEU annually carried by Team Lines linking Gdynia with Bremen/Bremerhaven and Hamburg using two vessels of 130/180 TEU twice weekly. Maersk also has a feeder link to Rotterdam with a capacity of 884 TEU weekly. Other notable links are provided to the United Kingdom by EuroAfrica and United Baltic (each weekly), to Eire, West Africa and the Mediterranean (by POL subsidiaries) and to the Far East by Chipolbrok a state-owned Chinese/Polish joint venture.

Meanwhile recent moves from BCT, despite the impending capacity problems, include taking a part share in the Polish block train operator Speedcont who provides regular connections to and from the main industrial centres of Warsaw, Łódź, Kraków, Sosnowiec, Malaszewicze, Wrocław and Poznań, with the aim of increasing feeder movements through the port. In the first year of operation in 1995, these trains moved 5700 containers, with an increase to more than 10000 in 1996 and 30000 in 1997 utilising 10 trains a week. Plans for new equipment and improved storage and movement systems for the containers will allow expansion up to 220000 TEU per annum, but further increases hinge on the acquisition of navy land adjacent to the current site giving an additional 250 metres of berthing capacity.

As with all the new operating companies, BCT is owned by the Port Authority at the moment but privatisation is expected to begin in 1997 following the adoption of the new government regulations for ports allowing and facilitating the further separation of port operations and management.

A new development in 1997 was the agreement with Daewoo Korean car manufacturer to import car kits for assembly in Warsaw through the container port rather than use other ports to the west in Germany or beyond. Meanwhile, one other initiative of BCT is its combined shipping service with POL America and C. Hartwig Gdynia - Baltic Container Lines - serving Gdynia, Hamburg and Bremerhaven. A seven day port rotation is achieved using three vessels (of 150 TEU each) providing an alternative to the truck and rail modes east - west across Europe. Some 31000 TEU were carried in 1996 and plans exist to extend the service to Rotterdam.

(2) Baltic Grain Terminal (BGT)

The Baltic Grain Terminal is used largely for the discharge of imported cereals and has been completely renovated with modern computer technology since the political and economic changes that took place at the end of the 1980s. It has the capacity to accommodate ships up to 245m in length and up to 13.5m draft resulting in a capability of discharging Cape-size bulkers up to 145000 DWT. Profits for 1996 were around US$1 million.

Further plans include developments in operating facilities to increase throughput to 3 million tonnes per annum. Cargoes are now regularly handled from countries in central Europe and the Czech Republic in particular. Imported grains include wheat, maize and soya, whilst the limited exports include rape seed meal, rape seed, wheat and rye. Both rail and road connections are provided. In May of 1997, the latest development in the grain terminal opened with a new 14000 tonne capacity silo costing 8m new złotys and destined for use in the grain and fodder market including trade within Poland and transit countries. This has raised capacity to over 25000 tonnes.

This development included the modernisation of the existing 1937 silo and the installation of a large number of new technological improvements to the grain handling systems. Further development projects include deepening of berths to allow a maximum draught of 12.7 metres.

An indication of the diversification inherent in the new terminals in Gdynia under the new regime, is the regular handling of exports of liquid urea ammonia nitrate fertiliser to the USA and Western Europe and also, discharging alumina at the grain terminal.

(3) Baltic General Cargo Terminal Gdynia Ltd (BTDG)

The Baltic general cargo terminal was set up by the Gdynia Port Authority on the 1st August 1995 providing handling, stevedoring and warehousing services and facilities for general cargo as well as providing a series of other highly specialised tasks. It has some 4300 metres of quayside, a maximum water depth of 12.10 metres, 75 cranes from 3 to 16 tonnes capacity, 29 mobile cranes, 165000 square metres of warehousing and 162000 square metres of open storage. Its workforce consists of 1100 people, the majority of whom are stevedores who work a 24 hour shift system, increasingly unhindered by demarcation disputes or regulations and continuously trained to improve efficiency, quality and productivity. There is also a bonded warehouse facility within the terminal area.

BTDG's activities at the moment are rather restricted by the limited activities of the port in general in the conventional cargo field and by the overall downward trend world-wide in general (rather than containerised) cargo. 1.7 million tonnes were handled in 1995, consisting primarily of steel products and soda. A limited amount of paper is handled for export and 100000 tonnes of bananas were imported in 1996 with plans for an improved and extended temperature controlled fruit import terminal. Destination markets are primarily European with limited connections to and from South America and the Far East.

Future plans at the terminal include extending market involvement in particular to Russia and other ex Soviet Union countries; combating the wide decline in general cargoes by introducing a duty free zone within which value can be added to products; developing a packaging terminal to repack bulk commodities arriving by road into smaller units; dredging projects to increase drafts from 11.30 metres to 12.80 with the potential of attracting bigger quantities of steel exports.

The terminal made a loss in 1996, but anticipated a profit in 1997.

(4) Morski Terminal Masowy Gdynia (MTMG)

Dry bulk cargoes comprise the biggest sector of Gdynia's throughput, representing over 3 million tonnes in 1995 and rising to 3.5 million tonnes in 1996. Of that, some 650000 tonnes were liquid bulk and 1.72 million tonnes were coal including the import of 300000 tonnes from Russia. This coal total represented a fall in volumes from 2.94 million tonnes in 1995. MTMG is responsible for handling all the dry bulk cargo in Gdynia since its formation. In particular, coal is the major commodity handled, exported to a large number of European countries, although increasingly exports of coke and coke-breeze are involved. These latter two commodities now represent over half of all the exports through the terminal. The coke-breeze is specifically exported to Spain.

One aspect of this concentration on the coal based market is a recognition by the terminal company that the commodity is in long term decline and, as a consequence, there is a need to search out new markets. Very limited quantities of chemicals are handled at the moment and the company hopes to expand this sector with particular reference to the Former Soviet region. Other projects include developing the soya, stones and aggregates sectors, and investment in new equipment, some of which has already occurred for coal based products.

MTMG employs around 500 people, of whom about 50 are administrative personnel. Additional labour is bought in from other terminals as and when required. The company hopes to attract both local and foreign investors at the earliest possible time and thus to move forwards to full privatisation at the earliest possible moment.

Other restructuring moves

The Port of Gdynia has taken further steps to move operations and management of the port towards independence, self-reliance and eventually privatisation. A number of harbour services previously offered by the port itself have now been converted into limited liability operations. These include:

(1) Portowy Zakład Transportu Sp. z.o.o. (Port Transport Co. Ltd.)

This is a wholly independent firm owned by the port concentrating upon providing transport services for the port and the repair and maintenance of vehicles.

(2) Portowy Zakład Techniczny Sp. z.o.o. (Port Technical Co. Ltd.)

This offshoot is responsible for the repair and maintenance of all types of cranes, electrical equipment, handling equipment and various diesel engine installations. Ancillary activities include ventilation and heating engineering work, painting and building repairs, roofing and security equipment installation and maintenance. Plans include ship and barge repair programmes.

(3) Przedsiębiorstwo Usług Żeglugowych i Portowych Gdynia Sp. z.o.o. (WUZ) (Shipping and Port Services Gdynia Co. Ltd.)

WUZ is a wholly owned limited liability subsidiary of the Port of Gdynia SA, and concentrates upon towing, shipping and port support functions within the Gdynia harbour area. It also undertakes ice breaking, pontoon transport and various other related services. The company inherited a wide range of equipment from the Port Authority including some nine tugs, three mooring boats, two pontoons, 13 barges, two floating cranes and a floating warehouse. Future plans include developing and providing services outside of the Gdynia port area for a range of customers.

(4) Portowy Zakład Zaopatrzenia Sp. z.o.o. (Port Supply Co. Ltd.)

Dating from mid 1995, the Port Supply Co. is responsible for the procurement of spare parts, acts as a consultancy office for companies within the port area and also acts as a documentation office. It is expected to be one of the first companies to be privatised under the new structure. Current developments include acting as procurement agents for any company that wishes to use them, whether connected with the port activities or not and evidence of this trend has emerged already with the signing of a contract to act as the distribution office for a tyre manufacturer.

Future plans

The Port of Gdynia has considerable plans for the immediate future which they intend to build upon the changes in structure, ownership and organisation that have been achieved already.

Plans exist for the further development of the 33 hectare duty free zone in the central and eastern part of the port - a natural development from the creation of Special Economic Zones created under the law of 1994 of which two specifically related to the port's activities already exist - associated with

Dalmor Deepsea Fishing Co. and the Gdynia Shipyard SA. Two further "distri-parks" are planned in close proximity to the ferry terminal.

Strategic port projects include a new fertiliser export terminal in the eastern port with a capacity of 300000 tonnes of both liquid and of dry cargo to be developed before the end of 1998 - this plant will be a joint venture between the port and Zakłady Azotowe Puławy, a Polish fertiliser manufacturing company; an oil products terminal; a new cement import terminal and packaging plant costing US$5 million, with an annual capacity of 200000 tonnes and storage of 10000 tonnes which was completed in September 1997 for the Swedish cement company Scancem; a series of distri-parks in collaboration with the renewed container and ro-ro facilities; additional grain storage facilities and the construction of new grain elevators and deepening of approach routes to accommodate 70000 tonne vessels with a full load; and a new dedicated alumina terminal (with a throughput of 200000 tonnes annually and storage of 5000 tonnes) as well as major developments in the ro-ro terminal for two new combined road/rail berths and two road only ones. These last ro-ro developments are related to the construction of new motorways in the region linking into the Trans European Network connecting Scandinavia through Poland to the Balkans and the Near East; Gdynia is the most suitably located of all the Polish ports for these ro-ro links, due to the proximity of the port facilities to the Gdynia expressway. According to external consultants reports of 1997, around 2.3 million tonnes of cargo will follow the Gdynia - Karlskrona route by 2010. This will include rail traffic for the first time if these planned developments take place resulting in around 1.6 million tonnes by road and 700000 tonnes by rail. This is a major expansion on the 1995 figures of 830000 tonnes by road and none by rail. External funding is a requirement for all these projects given the current and immediate condition of the Polish economy generally and the ports sector specifically.

However, the major aim for the future is one associated with privatisation. The new ports legislation, passing through parliament in 1996-7, will provide the basis for the sale of the spin-off companies noted above, which were once the operating sections of the port authority, leaving the latter simply to manage and organise the port as a whole whilst retaining ownership of the port's land. Decisions upon the introduction of outside capital, foreign investors or others have yet to be made but will have to be faced in the very near future and may involve stock market listings. The port is confident that these privatisation moves will be popular and relatively easy to achieve now that the structure and current ownership of activities and facilities has been clarified (72).

Discussion

A number of interesting issues emerge from this outline of the Port of Gdynia and its activities in recent years.

In terms of the port's organisation and organisational structure, quite considerable changes can be seen to have occurred stimulated by a combination of state force and a recognition of need. Thus the new operating companies represent a major move from the old system of management and provide extensive opportunities for future privatisation and development of new markets and services. The latter is beginning to occur although, quite understandably, only slowly. Privatisation of the operating companies will follow, although the exact form is unknown - and there is no doubt that these privatised units have a good opportunity to prosper in the new economic climate. In contrast, the old port authority will remain in public hands - albeit somewhat different ones with the introduction of local city interests which at least should help to stimulate the organisation into being more locally responsive. This may restrict developments and hinder ideas that are potentially of benefit to the port and its users. The strategic argument that ports need to be in state hands remains predominant in Poland unlike elsewhere (e.g. UK) where port privatisation of management and ownership (including land) is increasingly common. Possibly time will tell, and with the potential success of the privatised operators, the authority could follow.

One major change in the port has been the growth in number of overseas users since the economic and political changes of the late 1980s exemplified by Maersk (container) Line and its weekly service to Denmark, the Netherlands, and Germany feeding into its international container line network. This trend will continue and will help to force the port authority to consider its future strategy with respect to markets and reorganisation.

The port is generally profitable (e.g. around old Zł600bn in 1993 and old Zł168bn in 1994), with the variation largely explicable by variations in coal and to a lesser extent, grain throughput. This does not, of course, take account of the indirect subsidies available from the state in the form of major infrastructural grants, and also those from overseas international bodies (e.g. the World Bank).

Overall, there is considerable activity in the ports sector typified by the action in the Port of Gdynia. However, Gdynia presents a rather less political profile than that of its neighbour Gdańsk with its shipyard problems (15). Much more action is soon to follow with further commercialisation steps and the inevitable march towards privatisation. In many ways this matches the steps already taken in the shipping sector with, for example, the creation of subsidiary companies in PZM and Polish Ocean Lines which are distanced from the parent but ready for further moves towards the private sector. This

last stage is a difficult one to accomplish but is increasingly becoming a fact
of life following the restructuring of port activities and ownership.

Zarząd Portu Gdańsk S.A. (Port of Gdańsk)

Introduction

The current situation in the port of Gdańsk is as much a product of history as of any formal or organised planning process. Gdańsk (Danzig under German control), spent much of the early twentieth century outside of any Polish territory that might exist at that time and although it has a history of port activity dating back to 997AD, it was largely neglected after 1900 until the 1950s because of a series of political and historical accidents.

In particular, following the first world war, the region around and including Gdańsk was deemed a free city separate from Polish territory (and in fact dominated by German control and interests) thus denying Poland itself a major seaport. Szczecin at this time was part of Germany proper (Stettin). The consequence was that Poland dedicated itself until after the conclusions of the second world war, to the construction and development of Gdynia which was located on the very narrow strip of Polish land adjacent to the Baltic Sea. Thus Gdańsk was neglected by the Poles, although some investment did follow from German interests, until the Communists decided to develop its facilities to complement Gdynia after 1947. Specialisation then became the overt policy and Gdańsk was chosen as the new bulk port for the country. Container developments were concentrated in Gdynia. Some form of spatial specialisation was also developed with Szczecin (now returned to Poland) concentrating more on the Scandinavian markets and Gdańsk on the Soviet and Finnish areas. All these decisions were taken by state authorities with little discussion with the ports themselves. The particularly localised nature of the spatial differentiation was explicable by the limited markets which Polish bulk products enjoyed in the Communist days which were dominated by those of the Soviet Union and its allies.

Certain current features of the port are those inherited from the old system including its virtual monopoly of oil imports, its lack of true container facilities, and its underused coal and ore facilities. It also displays all the features that both Gdynia and Szczecin/Świnoujście display as the process of port renewal and revitalisation takes place in Poland. Thus we shall see the reorganisation of the Port Authority, the creation of new operating companies and the rather unknown effects of the new ports legislation particularly concerning ownership, beginning to have an impact.

Gdańsk is a large port of 370 ha. of water and 662 ha. of land, 18 km of quay of which 9.9 km is commercially used. Some 85000 sq. metres of covered and 545000 sq. metres of open storage is available. It is divided as a port into two parts - the old port at the mouth of the River Wistula (the inner port) and the new Northern Port area (Port Polnocny). The inner port can receive vessels up to a length of 225m and a maximum draft of 10.2m corresponding to around 30000 DWT. The Northern Port has a maximum draft of 16.5m, and can accommodate ships of 300m length and up to 150000 DWT.

Port turnover

The cargoes handled at the port of Gdańsk are dominated by bulk commodities and in particular a limited number of specialisms which, as we have already seen, are largely a consequence of Communist controls and influence in the past fifty years. Totals for 1996 reached 16.5 million tonnes reflecting a decrease on the 15.5 million tonnes achieved in 1995 a reduction resulting from the decline in coal trade generally and the rise in oil prices at that time

Taking the trades of Gdańsk in some sort of order of importance and beginning with the most significant we can analyse the current pattern of turnover.

(1) Coal - is by far the most important commodity that moves through Gdańsk. Taking figures for 1995, 39% of all cargo throughput was coal representing some 7.1 m tonnes. This is a reduction on the figures for 1994 which in turn had reduced from 1993 and represents the effects of the decline in Polish coal exports generally. This decline has continued in the first half of 1996 (when first half figures reduced from 4.13m tonnes to 2.81m tonnes - some 32% less) and is beginning to have a notable impact on overall results. We shall see the port's response to these trends in a later section. The coal

terminal itself, is located in the new Northern Port and is fully automated to deal almost exclusively with industrial products with a storage capacity of 600000 tonnes and a daily throughput of 50000 tonnes. It is thus capable of handling considerably more than it now does and rather than suffering from a lack of investment, simply suffers from a changing international energy market.

(2) Liquid fuels - represented some 35.2% of cargo turnover in Gdańsk in 1995 and thus formed the second most important commodity. Unlike coal, which is also serviced through Szczecin, Gdańsk has an almost complete monopoly on oil movements into and out of Poland and thus can afford to be a little more relaxed in this market. It is also, of course, a rather more buoyant trade particularly in the light of the changing industrial requirements of Poland. To some extent this is countered by the intense efforts being made to reduce energy wastage and to transform Polish industry from its history of high energy consumption, heavy enterprises. Some 6.4 m tonnes were processed in 1995.

Liquid fuels is one of the rare sectors to inherit a major advantage from the old regime in that a well developed oil pipeline network exists and has existed for many years, connecting Gdańsk with, in particular, the Former Soviet Union and former East Germany (DDR). Current contracts include direct supply of the Schwedt and Leuna refineries in Germany of 4m tonnes of oil annually, rising eventually to 15m tonnes. Meanwhile, the fear of ex-Soviet problems in supplying oil through the "Friendship" pipeline encouraged the Polish government to invest heavily in oil processing facilities in Gdańsk through the establishment of Naftoport with the state companies of Gdańsk Refinery, Plock Petrochemia, Pern Pipeline, Polska Żegluga Morska (PZM) and the Central Oil Product Agency. Oil handling capabilities increased from 6m tonnes annually to between 12 and 13m tonnes so that domestic demands could be satisfied. Gdańsk thus finds itself in a relatively strong position processing a commodity in demand and with a virtual (domestic) monopoly.

The result of this collaboration has been the US$26.65m investment in the new Northern Port liquid fuels facility with two new berths for tankers up to 150000 DWT providing a total of 17m tonnes oil handling capacity per annum. In addition to this, a 25 year lease for a new gas terminal was agreed in 1994 following the signing of a $30m contract with gas importer and distributor Gaspol (partly owned by seven Polish gas distributors and partly by the Netherlands company SHV). The terminal will have an annual capacity of 500000 cu. m. and will cost around $22m in the first phase, opened in spring 1997 including 6000 tonnes tank facilities and a new loading berth. Current gas imports come through a temporary facility in the inner harbour.

(3) Other bulk - is the third largest category and includes a multitude of products representing some 15.1% of cargo and 2.8 m tonnes in 1995.

(4) General cargo - rather surprisingly, makes up the next largest category. Gdańsk has never developed a strong general cargo base for the historical reasons outlined earlier. Some 1.7 m tonnes were processed in 1995 representing around 9.5% of the turnover of the port. This figure, like coal, is in gradual decline and the Port Authority has a number of plans to turn this around which we shall discuss later in this chapter but centre around the development of both container facilities and the new Duty Free Zone. Liner operators are few in number and include Turkish Cargo to Izmir, Mersin, Istanbul and Derince; PNSC to Karachi in Pakistan and Dammam in Saudi Arabia; ENC to Alexandria in Egypt; and SC India to Bombay, Calcutta and Madras. Frequencies on any route do not exceed monthly.

(5) Other categories of cargo include the following commodities listed in the table below:

CARGO	MILLION TONNES 1995	%
Liquid sulphur	1.10	6.1
Phosphorites	0.30	2.0
Grain	0.14	0.8
Soda	0.13	0.7
Timber	0.07	0.4
Pulp	0.06	0.3
Construction timber	0.01	0.1

Source : Zarząd Portu Gdańsk SA, 1996

Vessel turnover

Some 2045 ships visited Gdańsk during 1995 with around 611 in the broad 'other' category - designated as shipyard visitors, passenger ferries, cargo ferries, bunkering ships and others - some 446 bulk carriers, 401 general cargo, 294 coal carriers, 214 tankers, 56 grain ships and 23 timber. The majority were in the range of 501-2000 nrt (some 962 vessels) with 150 over 15000 nrt. Of the 2045 ships in total, 400 were of Polish flag.

Company structure

Under the new legislation which controls the management of state ports in Poland, the structure of Gdańsk Port as an organisation has been revised. The company, with some 200 office and around 230 operational staff (e.g. security guards, technicians etc.), is now headed by the President of the Board who has working with him four Directors - for Administration, Finance, Commerce and the Technical aspects of the port. The Administration Director is responsible for personnel, employment policy, training (in a wide range of activities including foreign languages, accounting and finance, taxation, international arbitration and marketing), legal issues, port security and administration; the Finance Director for port finance and budgetary control, the introduction of a new stock control system, economic analysis of the port and its sector, accounting and property; the Commercial Director for port development, analysis of port competition, promotion of both the port of Gdańsk and Polish ports generally and marketing. The Commercial Department is also responsible for the new offices opened in Kaliningrad (Russia) and participation in a number of exhibitions and seminars in Poland and abroad; and the Technical Director for safety and environmental protection, supervision of technical investment including a variety of dredging and quay extension projects, and technical maintenance. This new structure reinforces the trends away from the old operational dominance of the Port Authority and has helped to move it more towards the marketing, development and financial priorities that currently direct port activities all aided by the introduction of a new computer based management system. It thus contributes to the progress slowly being made in Polish ports generally, towards their commercialisation and privatisation.

On signing by the President of the New Ports Act in late 1997, the ownership of Gdańsk passed from the State Treasury - the existing owners of all the major Polish ports - to a mix of the Treasury (51%), the local municipality (34%) and other interests (15%) thus leaving control of the port in state hands and yet encouraging local interests to develop and eventually privatise as much of the operations, management and infrastructure as possible. As in Gdynia and Szczecin, the new regime will facilitate a number of new reforms including giving the port management the right to set port dues, currently set by the State and fixed across all ports at the same level.

The port actually operates two representative offices abroad as a means of promoting its activities and encouraging traffic to pass through Gdańsk. The locations reflect the growing markets of the port as they are located in Kaliningrad in Russia and in Dusseldorf in Germany. The latter was opened in 1994 with responsibility for promoting the port in Germany, the Netherlands, Belgium and Switzerland. The Kaliningrad office only opened in November

1995 and has amongst its other functions, collaboration with the port of Kaliningrad for the storage and transfer of cargoes, promotion of the port of Gdańsk and most importantly, the eventual development and introduction of a Gdańsk - Kaliningrad shipping line to facilitate the movement of goods across the congested Polish - Russian border. Both representative offices are typical of the changing image and outlook of Polish ports and the recognition of activities beyond those of simple port operation.

Gdańsk has also implemented a process of developing separate and independent stevedoring companies, similar to Gdynia, in anticipation of the privatisation process that will follow in the near future. These companies will be established ready to be sold off at short notice. Seven companies were originally set up, (now eight), one for each of the major stevedoring activities or locations - for example, liquid sulphur, the Westerplatte area of the port, Gorniczy Basin, crude oil etc. Each company, originally owned by the Port Authority, is now owned by the employees themselves with clear incentives to show commitment to their work area. Most appear to be operating well, except for the general cargo company where the decline in traffic from the Communist directed days, has been significant. Although losses in this company are high, the number of staff is largely retained through some sort of cross compensation operating between the other companies and the Port Authority.

Gdańsk claims to be profitable; for example, in 1995 a net profit of some 8.790m new złoties was made (around US$ 3-3.5m) which was very slightly less than in 1994 (new złoties 8.799m). The major growth areas were in operations in the port and growth in financial activities. However, taxation payments grew substantially as well. Less promising was the 9.7% fall in tonnes handled between 1995 and 1996 although this looked to have been turned around with a 14% rise in volumes in the first half of 1997. This growth was largely attributable to coal and liquid bulk commodities.

New developments and plans for the future

The port of Gdańsk is extremely active in the design of new plans and in the execution of a number of new projects, none of which would have been possible without the political, social and economic changes in Poland, nor the recent legislative developments which have occurred and which are about to markedly affect the Polish ports sector. All move the port towards a more commercial basis with the ultimate aim of full privatisation at some date in the future and in the immediate period, continued moves towards commercialisation.

(1) The Duty Free Zone

The Duty Free Zone (DFZ) at the Port of Gdańsk, is one of the ideas that has developed within the new environment that exists for international ports in East Europe as a whole and Poland rather more specifically. Gdańsk was the first of the three ports in Poland (the others being Gdynia and Szczecin/Świnoujście), to establish a free zone under State order on the 28th November 1995 (Legislation No. 141, Art. 693) with the DFZ opening in September of 1996. The zone is located at the port entrance to the sea on Władysława IV Quay and has a total land area of 33.5 ha with some 38000 sq. m. of covered storage, backed up by another 80000 sq. m. of open storage (34). The total quay length is 850m. comprising six berths able to accommodate ships up to a length of 174m. Maximum draft for vessels is 8.4m.

The principle aim of the new DFZ is of course, to attract new traffic to the port, but there is a particular and specific aim to attract traffic to and from the Former Soviet Union and Russia in particular as the locational and other benefits of Gdańsk, compared with ports in the Baltic States and Russia itself, are clearly apparent - e.g. better levels of security, ice free access and relatively well organised logistical facilities.

Under the new legislation, the following activities may be carried out in the DFZ by Polish, overseas and international companies:

> cargo handling
> cargo storage
> manufacturing
> product assembly
> forwarding and transport
> insurance
> consultancy

The advantages the DFZ presents over and above the rest of the Port of Gdańsk (but in common with other DFZs for example in Gdynia), consist of the following:

> - payment of customs duties and VAT deferred until the goods enter Polish customs territory;
> - waived customs guarantee payments;
> - reduced customs duties and VAT liabilities on goods processed in the DFZ;
> - increased security (CCTV, guards, fence and floodlighting).

Marketing strategies also emphasise the advantages in terms of access to both central European and Polish markets, and the security and quality provision over and above that of Russian Baltic ports.

The DFZ took some months to establish after the initial announcement and by early 1997 there was still no evidence of economic activity although the infrastructure was in place. In association with the objective of accessing Russian markets through the DFZ, has been the development of the proposed Kaliningrad shipping link and the regional representative offices opened there, providing safe and reliable communications via the DFZ with commodities never actually entering Polish customs territory but naturally enough, providing a source of income for the port, in particular if reprocessing could be included in the package. One easily identifiable problem is the lack of a tradition in the container markets for Gdańsk as a whole (as all containers were directed through the Baltic Container Terminal in Gdynia under the old regime) which has so far, constrained the ambitions of the Port Authority and the DFZ in establishing liner links. The DFZ management are also well aware of the need to improve their own logistical links if they are realistically to attract trade for transit to and from the east. To this end, western consultants from the UK have been employed to develop trade and to assess strategies for the future.

By July 1997, the new DFZ had attracted more than 35 customers and was continuing to market the facility as an alternative to Gdynia's facility and with particular reference to transit trade with the CIS and steel, timber and container traffic.

(2) Ore and grain terminal development

A new iron ore terminal covering some 30 ha. is to be developed by Polish owned steel mills Huta Katowice, in collaboration with Brazilian iron ore exporters. Capacity will be around 3-5m tonnes p.a. with construction underway in early 1997 and completion sometime in 1998. The Northern port already possesses an ore quay, as we noted earlier, but which lies dormant as far as ore is concerned and is used solely for a variety of steel products. Eventually it is hoped that not only Polish but Slovak and Czech importers could use the new facility. Total investment is expected to exceed US$50m.

Agreement has also been reached with Europort (Canada/USA) to create a new grain terminal with a capacity of between 2-4 million tonnes p.a. for imports located on a 20 year old Soviet built iron ore pier facility (33). Conversion would depend upon a 25 year lease on the pier and a 12 year exclusion rights for grain handling. Agreed initially in May 1995, the objective is to attract larger vessels that usually trade through Hamburg and the terminal will include facilities for processing feedstuffs as well, and will take up about 56ha of the port area. The main market targets area here are the FSU countries and to provide sufficient capacity for them, storage for around 150000 tonnes of grain will be provided with equipment to facilitate loading/unloading at 750 tonnes per hour using a 300m berth with a depth of 16.5m. The second phase of the project would relate to the feedstuffs and fertiliser side including two more berths and facilities for urea export. A further stage would include additional cranes and storage facilities. Total cost is estimated at about US$145m.

Investors in the consortium include the Saskatchewan Wheat Pool, which would manage the facility, Dessaport International, a Halifax (Canada) based engineering company, and a USA based development company. Application for permission to develop the facility was lodged in May 1997 with an anticipated start date of November that year and completion some two years later.

(3) Liquid fuels and coal terminal development

Development of a new LPG terminal began in 1995 and was completed in Spring 1997. Here the main objective is the import of petrol from Norway in minimum amounts of 800000 tonnes p.a.. The project is financed by the jointly owned UK, Dutch, and Polish company Gaspol which possesses a 75% market share of Polish petroleum products in a very fast growing market. Meanwhile, the construction of a third oil pier in the port will, with the other developments in this sector, bring the capacity of Gdańsk up to 35m tonnes p.a. of liquid fuels. Much of this growth is based upon the inherited and extensive pipeline network put in place by the old regimes in Poland, the Soviet Union and the DDR. Gdańsk is able to supply directly, the German refineries of Schwedt and Leuna at highly competitive rates. 17m tonnes of this liquid fuel capacity is for oil handling, providing plenty of room at present for Polish needs and transit traffic. Some 4m tonnes moves annually to Germany through an agreement with Naftoport. Total investment should be around US$23m.

(4) Highway development

One of the major infrastuctural developments in Poland occurring at the moment and as a direct response to the economic changes that have taken place in the 1990s, is the planned improvement of the highway network. Under the old regime, highways were considered very secondary in status and importance after the rail network for inland distribution and received little funding reflected still today in their low quality and inadequate capacity for modern logistical needs. The port access roads were no exception to this general rule, and in the north of the country, following the social, political and economic changes of the late 1980s, there were no motorways and few dual carriageway facilities. Road surfaces were inadequate, road signing poor, drainage of low quality and other facilities (e.g. services, lighting and safety provision) were substandard. Through the 1990s, plans were developed for the improvement of road facilities and in the Gdańsk (and Gdynia) area the new A1 motorway has been proposed and designed to improve access to the ports and to link the Tricity of Gdańsk, Gdynia and Sopot, with Warsaw and beyond. Unfortunately, although the physical planning is complete, there remain difficulties in attracting private investment through the assembly of a consortium and agreement of the precise financial arrangements, necessary as the Polish state cannot afford to build these new roads without it, and international governmental investors (e.g. the European Union) are unprepared to finance them alone. Once the financial arrangements can be at least partially agreed, there will be a public tendering process to select the preferred consortium bidder. Additional highway improvements will include new links to the Gdańsk by pass and the nearby airport at Rębiechowo to be financed by the World Bank (14).

In addition to this major motorway development, which incidentally will form part of the Trans European Motorway between Scandinavia and southeast Europe and Turkey, utilising the ferry links that currently serve Gdańsk and Gdynia, funding has been agreed again with the World Bank and the Polish Ministry of Transport in October 1996, for the construction of a new 1400m road bridge over the River Wistula to the east of the city eventually linking in with the new motorway system and a variety of connecting highways that will improve access to the port and relieve local congestion. A whole new area of the port, to the south east of other developments, will then be opened up for container and ro-ro traffic which is currently almost non-existent in Gdańsk. The new bridge will be finished by 1999 at a cost of US$26m. This fits in nicely with the anticipated container capacity problems for Gdynia from around 2002. The Baltic Container Terminal in Gdynia has no room for expansion because it is surrounded by the city itself and with the growth of the Polish and FSU economies it is expected that container traffic, in particular, will expand substantially.

(5) Other Developments

A variety of other developments in the port are either underway or proposed. These include a cement and asphalt plant in connection with the expansion of the Polish road building programme; a new malt factory, funded to the tune of 14m DEM and owned by German interests plus the International Finance Corporation which should be completed during 1998 and will provide 50% of output for Polish consumption and 50% for export - annual capacity will be 120000 tonnes of malt from 170000 tonnes of barley; new pier facilities funded by the Port Authority, for which, as yet (1997), there are no designated purposes but which openly display confidence in the port; further liquid chemical developments which although expected to cause some environmental problems and meet environmental resistance, are likely to be attracted to Gdańsk where sites are available, unlike Gdynia where the proximity of the city makes such developments impossible; and roll on-roll off ferry developments which, at present remain very insecure. Recent (1996) loss of the Helsinki service because of a failure to use an appropriate ship orientated towards a freight market and thus disappointing loadings, has left Gdańsk with only the (PZB) Oxelsund/Nynashamn route which runs three times weekly in the winter and daily in the summer. However, the Gdańsk ferry terminal operated by a separate semi-private company - Sirkopol (in effect PZB, the state ferry company), is both old and small and in need of urgent replacement in particular to facilitate the use of modern, larger ferries. Plans exist for its redevelopment at the Obroncow Westerplatte Quay, costing US$2m and includes new parking facilities for trucks and some additional highway improvements.

Discussion

There is considerable developmental activity in the Port of Gdańsk, which reflects the sizeable political, economic and social changes that have occurred in Poland and more specifically, the impact of commercialisation and potential privatisation in the ports sector. The creation of a series of new stevedoring companies in a form suitable for privatisation at short notice reflects the attitude of the port towards the future and is mirrored, to a certain extent, by the number and range of new port projects that are either proposed or actually in a state of development. Inevitably, some of these proposals will never see the light of day as the funding that they need may not be available and the markets to which they are directed may never emerge. However, the sheer volume and number of projects implies a faith in the future of the port and a recognition that change must and will occur. No longer can Gdańsk survive on the limited markets it was once allocated and there is a pressing need to improve the physical facilities of those existing market sectors and to begin to direct energies towards new ones.

The new ownership structure of the port, resulting from the new Port Act which came in to force during 1997, will push the Port Authority itself further down the line towards privatisation, matching the moves of the stevedoring companies. Gdańsk will at least possess the basis for this privatisation and has recognised the new spatial markets that it needs to enter including those with enormous potential in the Former Soviet Union and the Kaliningrad enclave, the Baltic States and Belarus in particular. Polish sources of trade - either import or export - cannot support the level of activity in any of the existing Polish international ports (Gdańsk, Gdynia or Szczecin/Świnoujście) that would be needed to provide a profitable base, and thus to survive the rigours of privatisation, new markets must be found. However, some doubt has to be expressed about the likely possibilities of Gdańsk achieving a viable level of trade particularly in the general cargo markets where Gdynia's pre-eminence in the container trades makes progress elsewhere very difficult. This is even with the anticipated and widely acknowledged growth in container trades that is bound to occur with the gradual, and inevitable, growth of the economies of central and eastern Europe. Similar comments can be made about the roll on-roll off ferry market, where considerable growth again can be anticipated with the developments in Central and Eastern Europe, the integration of Sweden and Finland into the European Union and the eventual construction and opening of the Trans European Motorway network in southern and eastern regions of the continent. Gdynia's advantage in current facilities, and its locational advantage nearer the open Baltic Sea unconstrained to a narrow site with outdated facilities, may mean that developments in Gdańsk are very difficult to encourage. The loss of the growing Helsinki market is indicative of the problems that are faced.

Some comments can also be made about the relationship that exists between the new stevedoring companies and the Port Authority. In theory there is no conflict. The new companies are independent of the authority and must make profits to survive at least in the long term, adapting to market conditions and opportunities as they see fit. In practice, there is undoubtedly some form of cross-subsidy going on to ensure that those stevedoring operations who have inherited the less fortunate areas of activity - for example general cargo - remain supported by the more active ones (for example the coal and oil terminal workers). Despite Port Authority claims that each stevedoring company retains its own profits and can go bankrupt, there seems to be an active process of support to ensure that this does not take place which cannot continue with full privatisation. In addition, the Port Authority claims to negotiate appropriate leasing charges for services and equipment which ensure that the stevedoring companies do not go bankrupt - in other words they are treated favourably - because they constitute old employees of the port. As new (private) companies emerge who wish to lease equipment (for example), they are treated more "economically realistically". Some doubt has to be raised about the merits of this sort of approach within a free market situation in the ports industry of Poland as a whole where the competitive environment is becoming increasingly apparent and unavoidable.

In addition to these problems, the port has also expressed concern over its inability to attract credit from both domestic and international institutions because of its new structure and the large number of small operating units that now exist. This may present problems in the future for the other Polish ports as well.

Finally two issues; firstly, considerable hopes are pinned upon the new Duty Free Zone. However, Gdańsk, as with all Polish ports, is a very late entry into this market in the Baltic region as a whole and may find it difficult to prove attractive over and above established competitors and those new competitors emerging all the time in locations such as St Petersburg, the Baltic States, the new revitalised eastern länder of Germany and even Poland itself (e.g. Gdynia). Secondly, the political significance of Gdańsk as a port location should not be overlooked and the 1997 troubles relating to the bankrupt shipyard are indicative of this (35, 36).

Zarząd Portu Szczecin Świnoujście S.A. (Port of Szczecin Świnoujście)

Introduction

Szczecin-Świnoujście Port represents the third of the large international ports of Poland that we will discuss, following the sections on Gdynia and Gdańsk which were included earlier. The previous Communist regimes had designated these three locations as those for the export and import of international cargo, along with a limited number of inland and domestic services, international passenger and vehicle ferry operations and substantial shipbuilding, ship repair and maritime ancillary activities. To this day they monopolise this sector having inherited the facilities and market advantages from the old regime which has naturally precluded the development of new competitors from within Poland. Competition remains fierce between them within Poland and from ports in Germany, the Netherlands, Italy, the Baltic States and Russia.

Szczecin-Świnoujście today is a major bulk port specialising in coal, iron ore and grain but with substantial interests in a multitude of other bulk commodities, general (non unitised) cargo and ferry traffic (75). In total there are some 8 km of quays and over 130 cranes and the port can handle ships with a draught of up to 12.8 metres at Świnoujście and 9.15 metres at Szczecin. These draught differences reflect the fact that Świnoujście is located at the mouth of the Odra River on the Baltic Sea whilst Szczecin is located some 53 km up the Odra River, close to the German border and on an inland waterway route to Berlin and beyond across Europe (61).

The very first merchant vessel did not enter Szczecin harbour until after the end of the second world war in 1946 when both sea and inland navigation were commenced following the inheritance of the town of Stettin from the

Germans - subsequently renamed Szczecin. At this time little was left of the city following extensive war damage - this included destruction of 80% of the port infrastructure, 90% of the shipyards, 60% of sea fishing equipment and facilities, between 60 and 80% of the textiles industry, 93% of metallurgical industries, 90% of chemical industries, 80% of food processing industries, 80% of the power supply sector and large proportions of the sanitation, water and gas networks. The initial shipping service was one provided by the Polish Baltic Coastal Trade Company concentrating on services between Szczecin and Świnoujście; regular sea navigation services started in 1947. Shipbuilding also commenced around this time in 1948 and continues in the same basic location to this day, whilst ship repair work started from 1950.

From this time until 1991 and following the economic, political and social changes of the late 1980s, Szczecin steadily grew as a location for shipping related activities but operated as part of the state as a designated port authority - effectively a state department - in similar fashion to Gdynia and Gdańsk. In May 1991, the port authority was restructured by the government into a state owned joint stock company (in a similar fashion to Polish Ocean Lines and PZM) and at the same time the company was reorganised into a port authority with responsibilities for management and land ownership and for 17 new operating companies, where some 55% of the shares were owned by employees of each of the companies and the remaining 45% by the state. (75)

The intention here was to lay the ground for the first stages of privatisation, which as we shall see, are now in 1997 beginning to see taking full effect. However, in 1994 the port authority recognised that the 17 operating company strategy was too fragmented and as a result they reduced the number of companies to 10, which we shall examine later but which consisted of a mix of stevedoring, ship operating, infrastructure, port repair and employee enterprises.

Overall, the new port authority, which remained at that stage 100% state owned, acted merely as a facilitator for these enterprises encouraging and allowing them to develop in the private sector. The 45% state ownership that remained was held by the port authority who thus retained an active interest in the activities and progress that was made. This structure, in late 1997, has just changed.

Privatisation

As we have already seen Szczecin-Świnoujście port, along with the ports of Gdynia and Gdańsk, has already taken the first steps towards entering the private sector. These first steps were taken in the Autumn of 1990, not long after the transformation phase of the late 1980s, and followed an intense period of reorganisation within the port, in particular delegating authority and functions to the existing operating units from the port authority itself, and simplifying the process of policy-making and decision-making.

In the following year in May, the port authority became the first Polish port and one of the first state enterprises in the region to be transformed into a "State Treasury" company with 100% of shares owned by the state, a vital and necessary first step towards privatisation. The port authority became a holding company - 100% state owned - which had responsibility for and part ownership (some 45%) of the 17 operating units which were established, each with limited liability and legally and organisationally independent. The remaining 55% was owned by those of the workforce prepared and able to invest in the companies. However, in 1994 these companies were reduced to 10, to achieve a combination of economies of scale and a more rational approach to management and operations.

The aim of the privatisation process was to decentralise the system of management within the organisation and to begin to form a more streamlined and effective structure. Each of the new operating companies now undertakes their activities at their own risk and according to their own policies and decisions. Their relationship to the newly formed port authority holding company is regulated by Polish commercial law and also reinforced by a formal civil agreement between the sides. The operating companies are thus responsible for all the day to day running of the activities of the port within the broader structure and policy of the port authority. The ownership pattern of the port authority has now very recently changed in late 1997, which we shall examine in a later section, but essentially, the relationship between the two sets of bodies remains the same.

In time it is expected that the operating companies will become further exposed to the privatisation process, going beyond the original concept of buyouts by the employees and managers and encouraging more investment from outside industry including at some time, investment potentially by international and foreign companies. Each of these operating companies is already a joint stock company and thus in a position to develop into a fully fledged private enterprise as time passes. The advantages that this will bring are seen as those that privatisation always has the potential to bring - in increased financial and economic discipline, flexibility and responsiveness to the market and diversification.

New port structures

As with both Gdynia and Gdańsk, Szczecin-Świnoujście Port Authority has been subject to the impact of the new Ports Act of Poland which, after a very long gestation period finally came into force in August of 1997. Part of the delay in passing this Act stemmed from a long running argument within the Szczecin-Świnoujście port concerning the desire by Świnoujście to be designated a separate and independent port authority of its neighbour based on its substantial activities particularly in the bulk and ferry trades. This argument was eventually resolved in favour of a combined authority but a lot of time passed whilst the discussions (and others) took place.

The new Ports Act structure essentially changes the ownership structure of the Polish ports industry and in particular pushes the path of privatisation along further for the port authorities. From August 1997, the port authority has now become 51% owned by the state Treasury, 24.5% Szczecin City Authority and 24.5% Świnoujście City Authority rather than the 100% state owned situation that existed before. Hardly a major step forward for privatisation but it does imply and suggest two things:

- greater local interest in the running of the port and thus a move towards more local responsiveness and a better understanding of the needs, problems and opportunities that might exist. It is hoped, albeit implicitly, that this might include investment by the local cities in the port.

- the opportunity for the port owners to sell off the port to other interested buyers if they wish and thus to attract investors from private industry, the local maritime community and overseas.

It is notable that the state has retained a majority interest in the port authority and thus has the ability to veto any privatisation moves of which it does not approve. Ports remain viewed as strategic entities - at least to a certain extent - by the government and are unlikely to be sold off to any sort of private sector investor without explicit state assessment first.

The port authority will remain non-profit making for the moment. The immediate first effect was the impact that the restructuring might have on the port's internal structure and organisation. This remained unclear in late 1997. In addition, there were rumours that the operating companies might be the first to invest in the new port authority thus reinforcing the general pattern of incestuous ownership that permeates the Polish maritime sector.

Under the new structure, in immediate terms the internal structure of the port authority organisation remains the same and remarkably simple. It consists of an Executive Board with three members - President, Technical Director and Economic and Finance Director. Closely associated with this Board is the Marketing and Development Director. The authority's activities follow from this structure.

With the new ownership structure, there will be a new board which will include representatives of the state, the local cities and other shareholders as they join. Current (1997) employee levels are around 530 in the port authority and some 3700 in the operating companies of which the majority are shareholders.

The operating companies

Some ten port operating (or service) companies have been established under the port authority and which are the enterprises that have been privatised and as time goes on, are expected to become further detached from the work of the port authority umbrella organisation. These companies are outlined in the following sections.

(1) Bulk Cargo Port Szczecin Sp. z.o.o.

This company is divided into three parts comprising the cargo port terminal, the coal port terminal and the MAS port terminal, all three of which are located in Szczecin.

The *cargo port terminal* specialises in steel products, general cargo, timber and other selected bulk cargoes utilising four quays scattered across the port of Szczecin. The terminals have some 150000 sq. metres of open storage and covered storage of 10000 sq. metres, the latter used exclusively for timber and general cargo. The *coal port terminal* specialises in the handling and storage of coal and some other bulk cargo and a variety of other general cargoes and operates from four quays all located close together in the port of Szczecin. Finally, the *MAS port terminal* is a multi-purpose terminal operation handling in particular, ores and their concentrates, some coal and a number of other bulk and general cargoes. It operates from three quays all located in close proximity in the port of Szczecin.

(2) Drobnica-Port Szczecin Sp. z.o.o.

This company specialises in general cargo but has active interests also in the traditional areas for Szczecin-Świnoujście, of bulk and grain handling. It operates three terminals - the *EWA-Stevedoring terminal* which constitutes two quays located adjacent to each other in the centre of Szczecin port and which specialises in general cargo including heavy lifts, roll-on/roll-off and lo-lo traffic. Container handling takes place here using specialised cranage facilities. Storage includes 18000 sq. metres covered and space for 200000 tonnes of cargo in the open. The *Łasztownia terminal* operates from five quays again situated in the centre of Szczecin port. Specialising in general cargo, it owns 64000 sq. metres of covered and a limited 16000 sq. metres of open storage. Specialisms include pest control facilities and the handling and storage of hazardous goods. There is also a bonded warehouse facility. Finally, there is the *Starówka terminal* which handles a mix of conventional general cargo, some bulk cargo, aggregates and liquid cargo that does not require heating. With only one quay located in central Szczecin port, it also consists of covered accommodation of 8484 sq. metres, open storage of 8050 sq. metres and a bonded warehouse.

(3) FAST Terminals Sp. z.o.o.

FAST is a joint venture between the Szczecin-Świnoujście Port Authority and the Belgian/UK company Fast Shipping Limited. The terminal comprises four adjacent quays located in the central area of Szczecin port which specialise in handling unitised general cargo, chemicals, timber and steel products. Facilities include a multi-purpose warehouse for general cargo of 8000 sq. metres, open storage areas of 35000 sq. metres and a variety of cranage facilities. The terminal is largely used as the Gdynia base for the regular shipping service that is operated by Fast Shipping between Szczecin and the UK ports of Tilbury, Howendyke and Perth and the Belgian port of Antwerp.

(4) Przedsiębiorstwo Usług Portowych Elewator EWA Sp. z.o.o.

The "Elevator Company EWA" specialises in the transhipment of grain, seed, animal feed pellets and other related products and operates from a single quay in the port of Szczecin utilising their own grain silo with a total capacity of 73000 cubic metres. Related equipment permits loading and unloading of shipments at a rate of 3600 tonnes of grain daily from or into rail wagons, or 4000 tonnes of grain or 2500 tonnes of soya beans a day to or from ships. In addition the company also operates a bonded warehouse facility.

(5) Port Handlowy Świnoujście Sp. z.o.o.

This company operates three terminals handling coal, iron ore, conventional general cargo and aggregates utilising a variety of cranes and having available a number of open storage areas including space for 120000 sq. metres of coal, 5200 sq. metres of iron ore, 8000 sq. metres of aggregates and also accommodation for general cargo. Four quays are utilised for these bulk shipments on the east bank of the Odra River in Świnoujcie in addition to a facility on the west bank for passenger and cruise ships.

(6) Zakład Usług Żeglugowych Sp. z.o.o.

This company does not operate terminals but is responsible for towage, mooring, other cargo handling services and transport by barge. Its fleet consists of a number and variety of port tugs, sea-going tugs, floating cranes for bulk cargo and a floating crane for heavy lift work. It is based in Szczecin but operates throughout the entire port and its approaches.

(7) PWCM-Navirem Sp. z.o.o.

PWCM is an engineering company that manufactures cranes, trailers, belt conveyors, cargo handling equipment and steel and aluminium structures. It also services and repairs existing equipment, structures and ships and can provide carpentry, engineering, welding and electrical skills. It is registered with the Polish Register of Shipping for the repair and quality control of containers. It operates a quay in the lower Odra part of Szczecin port.

(8) PZR-Port Crane Service Sp. z.o.o.

In a similar fashion to PWCM, PZR also maintains and repairs a variety of port equipment specialising in cranes, conveyors, electric motors, fork lift trucks, grabs and trailers. It also manufactures slings and high pressure, hydraulic ropes.

(9) Infra-Port Sp. z.o.o.

Infra-Port is a construction company specialising in building works for quays, port structures, roads, power and communication networks, pipe systems and water facilities. It also provides a road transport facility of trucks and cars.

(10) Doker-Port Sp. z.o.o.

Doker-Port covers a number of functions concentrating upon the supply of port manpower but also providing training facilities and repair services to port equipment

As can be seen from the above summary, there is some considerable overlap between many of the services provided and thus discussion of these services is best achieved by dealing with each main market of the port in turn. In particular, we will concentrate upon the provision of facilities for bulk and general cargo.

Bulk cargo

Bulk cargo forms the largest proportion of throughput at Szczecin-Świnoujście port which in turn represents the largest bulk port in the southern Baltic and by far the largest in Poland. Between them, Szczecin and Świnoujście handle some 18 million tonnes of bulk cargo a year including 40% of all Polish coal exports and 90% of all iron ore imports. However, although Szczecin plays a significant role in this activity, it is the berths in Świnoujście that forms the main location for bulk traffic activity. These berths were constructed by the Communist regimes in the 1960s and 1970s as a deliberate development policy in the region between state and region/city. The main commodities involved are coal, iron ore, sulphur, chemicals and aggregates.

Świnoujście can accommodate vessels up to Panamax size - i.e. 240 metres long, 12.8 metres draught and of 70000 DWT. Szczecin is far more constrained in that the maximum length vessel that can be accommodated is 210 metres with a 9.15 metres draught.

Coal as we have seen earlier, is the main commodity for the port and dominates in the Świnoujście complex. Both imports and exports are handled but the latter clearly dominate in the context of the Polish economy. However, imports are growing as cheaper sources become available - for example from the Former Soviet Union. Storage facilities in Świnoujście exceed 700000 tonnes whilst loading systems are capable of handling some 2000 tonnes per hour.

Some activity in the coal market also goes on in Szczecin commonly involving the use of rail trucks and barges. Although the activity is considerably less than at Świnoujście, Szczecin still has storage facilities for 200000 tonnes and can handle 1000 tonnes per hour.

Iron ore is the second most important commodity of the port and constitutes import traffic only. Virtually all this traffic comes in via quays in Świnoujście which are equipped with some of the largest, if not most modern, of handling equipment in the region. A limited quantity passes through a number of quays in Szczecin but constraints on ship size make this traffic less suitable for this inland river port.

Aggregates are also important and are concentrated through a new depot constructed in Świnoujście by Foster Yeoman of the United Kingdom for the transfer of Scottish materials for the markets in Germany. The depot accommodates self-discharging vessels of between 30000 and 70000 DWT and then tranships this cargo into barges for transfer to Germany by inland waterway using initially the Odra River and subsequently, the canal network of central Europe.

Other than this, there are notable facilities for grain and animal feed at the EWA Terminal as we have already seen, used for both import and export, and limited facilities in Szczecin at many of the general cargo terminals. In addition there are facilities for timber of all sorts including logs, sawn wood and pulp.

As we shall see later, much of the proposed development in the port relates to the bulk sector and the dominant position that it holds in the port.

General cargo

Despite this clear bulk dominance, general cargo remains an important source of trade in the port and has not been ignored by the authorities. Increasingly, the Port Authority has attempted to develop this sector as an alternative to the domination of bulk trades and as a means of diversifying their activities. Future plans include expansion and modernisation of facilities for general cargo including both conventional and unitised loads and its storage and transfer.

Szczecin already offers a full range of services for both lo-lo and ro-ro traffic, plus facilities for all types of general cargo in a variety of locations. A new specialisation has been the trade in steel products and facilities for their handling have recently been improved and extended. In addition there have been a number of developments of storage facilities for refrigerated products, hazardous cargoes and a large number of bonded warehouses, again scattered across the port.

However, general cargo, and in particular unitised cargo, has been hit by the modal changes that have followed the liberalisation of the freight transport market in Poland and with the increasing competition from trucking through Germany. Szczecin, clearly has problems in responding to this sizeable trend as the costs in both time and money of shipping such commodities by sea are commonly greater than by road. In a similar fashion, the ports of Hamburg, Bremen, Rotterdam and beyond are now much closer by truck than by sea and Szczecin has felt a serious loss in this trade during the 1990s.

Duty Free Zone

The Duty Free Zone in Szczecin-Świnoujście is the second attempt by the Port Authority to create a zone of this type following the bankruptcy of the first. This new zone was established by Government Ordinance of the 23rd August, 1994 and is administered by the Port Authority. Located in the general cargo area of Szczecin port, it covers some 4.49 hectares. In common with all Duty Free Zones in Poland, it constitutes a separate and uninhabited part of the Polish customs area that is considered as foreign territory where business activity can be performed by Polish, foreign and international economic units. All Polish laws apply to the area.

Scope of economic activities may include:

(1) cargo handling services including loading and discharging ships, storage in warehouses and open areas and cargo unitising;

(2) services to ships on entering and leaving port;

(3) social services to persons staying within the zone;

(4) goods related services;

(5) advisory services including legal, economic, forwarding, brokering and insurance activities;

(6) industrial and trading activities.

Polish customs have the responsibility of controlling the movement of goods and people across the borders of the Duty free Zone. There are no limits in terms of the value of goods that can pass into or out of the zone to and from foreign countries, nor are any dues charged. Taxation discounts are available to companies manufacturing or processing goods within the zone area.

Physical facilities include a 323m length and 7.5m draught quay, six rail mounted cranes of 3 tonnes capacity and a multi-storey warehouse of 20000 sq. metres situated on the quayside. Rail facilities are also available as are pest control facilities. The outside storage areas have recently been modernised with improved hard standing of 14000 sq. metres. The whole area is supervised and managed by a department of the port authority with the devolved power to issue permits, negotiate with customs and control the activities within the zone. Operational activities are concentrated, although not exclusively, within the remit of Drobnica-Port Szczecin Sp. z.o.o. - one of the privatised operations companies within the port noted earlier.

Transit cargo

Szczecin has always operated as transit port for central European countries by virtue of its geographical location, but also aided in the past artificially by the directed traffic principles of the former CMEA countries. Thus ex-Czechoslovakia was a notable partner in import and export trades over the years. In recent times, a combination of the loss of CMEA trade, a decline in ex-CMEA country economies, the rise in trucking as an alternative mode and the increasing desire for speedy transport services, have hit Szczecin as a port in terms of transit trade. It remains however, a serious aim of the port to regain and develop this market in the future - and it is by no means the case that all has been lost. The port remains at the cross roads of a significant east-west and north-south trade, including traffic between central Europe and Scandinavia, Germany, Austria and Denmark and this traffic is likely to grow as the European Union continues to expand and trade with the Middle Eastern countries develops. Polish entry to the EU can only help this trend. At present, the proximity of Szczecin to the border with Germany (and thus the EU) can only be helpful. Berlin, for example is only 135 km from Szczecin which remains its nearest major port.

Szczecin and Świnoujście remain linked to an extensive rail network that facilitates linkages to transit trade originating centres - particularly Vienna and Prague and also links to inland waterway systems that cross Europe. Unfortunately, the latter have tended to become seriously underused in recent years although traffic to and from Berlin - and in particular, aggregates - remains strong. Other waterway links serve areas of Poland but are little used. State plans exist to develop this inland waterway trade. In addition, Polish plans for motorway construction are soon to begin bearing fruit with the development of links south towards Poznań and the Czech Republic and west towards Berlin and Hamburg and east towards Gdańsk, the Baltic States and the Former Soviet Union.

Major transit partners in the mid 1990s are the Czech Republic, Slovakia and Germany (see Figure 23). The pattern of transit trade, albeit only over these two years of 1994 and 1995, shows a clear dominance of German traffic which in turn is dominated by the aggregates trade. This reliance on a single area is undesirable and is recognised by the port authority. In particular, it rests upon the reconstruction work currently being undertaken within the former German Democratic Republic (DDR) and which, by definition, has a finite life. Szczecin-Świnoujście port understands the need to diversify in transit trade to survive the inevitable changes that will follow.

Recent cargo throughput

A variety of statistics are available to examine recent cargo throughput of the complex as a whole but they vary in format and thus are difficult to present as a coherent whole. Figure 24 gives some idea of the growth of cargo since the end of the second world war and mainly under the Communist regime.

The dramatic fall in the throughput of the port following the political, social and economic changes of the late 1980s and early 1990s is clear from this set of data although to be fair, declining demand world-wide for coal also played a significant part in reducing the activities of the port. A general decline in most areas is apparent by 1990 - although the substantially high figure for grain in 1980 needs to be treated as a statistical anomaly derived from the

Figure 23
Transit cargoes via Szczecin-Świnoujście 1994 and 1995 ('000 tonnes)

Transit Country	Year	Coal	Iron Ore	Other Bulk	Grain	Timber	General Cargo	TOTAL
Czech	1994	208	54	13	0	13	890	1178
Rep	1995	105	216	9	0	11	306	692
Slovakia	1994	2	67	5	0	2	856	932
	1995	0	121	8	0	1	497	627
Germany	1994	4	305	292	0	0	143	744
	1995	3	286	303	0	0	153	745
Sea	1994	0	0	0	0	0	9	9
Transit	1995	0	0	0	0	0	8	8
Other	1994	0	0	0	0	0	4	4
	1995	0	0	0	0	8	6	14
TOTAL	1994	214	426	310	0	15	1902	2867
	1995	153	623	323	0	19	970	2088

Source: Szczecin-Świnoujście Port Authority, 1996.

Figure 24
Szczecin-Świnoujście port turnover 1946-1992 ('000 tonnes)

Year	Coal	Iron Ore	Grain	Timber	Other Bulk	General Cargo	TOTAL
1946	84	1	0	0	0	13	98
1955	3404	843	332	209	1220	764	6772
1965	4182	1428	992	288	2847	1762	11499
1974	12133	2685	752	369	4738	2439	23116
1980	9536	4762	2611	488	4221	3125	24743
1985	9116	3954	767	750	2401	2007	19055
1990	5845	2896	837	271	2164	2580	14593
1992	4939	1753	556	266	2230	2460	12204

Source: Szczecin-Świnoušjcie Port Authority, 1996

economic situation affecting Poland at the time (and the vagaries of Communist data).

Figure 25 gives an indication of the throughput of the port in more recent years - more specifically for 1994 and 1995 - but now divided up into the activities of the terminal operators rather than by commodity. As a result, variously different commodities are represented - although unspecified - in

Figure 25
Szczecin-Świnoujście cargo throughput 1994 and 1995

Operating Company	Year	Coal	Iron Ore	Other Bulk	Grain	Timber	General Cargo	TOTAL
Bulk Cargo	1994	4514	599	1234	6	92	850	7295
Pt Szczecin	1995	4383	695	1120	5	33	590	6826
%		97.1	116	90.8	83.3	35.9	69.4	93.6
Drobnica	1994	1	14	139	3	10	1400	1567
	1995	10	33	134	6	7	1120	1310
%		1000	235.7	96.4	200.0	70.0	80.0	83.6
FAST	1994	0	0	0	0	26	322	348
	1995	0	0	0	0	17	291	308
%		0	0	0	0	65.4	90.4	88.5
EWA	1994	0	0	0	261	0	0	261
	1995	0	0	0	587	0	0	587
%		0	0	0	224.9	0	0	224.9
Zaklad Us.	1994	0	0	21	0	0	0	21
Żeglug.	1995	3	0	18	0	0	0	21
%		-	0	85.7	0	0	0	100.0
Port Hand.	1994	4273	107	253	8	0	570	6175
Świnoujście	1995	3761	2394	235	34	0	93	6517
%		88.0	223.5	92.9	425.0	0	16.3	105.5
TOTAL	1994	8788	1684	1647	278	128	3142	15667
	1995	8157	3122	1507	632	57	2094	15569
%		92.8	185.4	91.5	227.3	44.5	66.6	99.4

Source: Szczecin-Świnoujście Port Authority, 1996

each of the terminal figures, depending upon the types of commodity each processed. As we noted earlier, many of the operators are very diverse in their markets and thus the figures do need to be treated with some caution.

Figure 26 gives the most up to date figures available for the port and indicate trends for the first half of 1997. Here we can see some recovery in the port from the decline in traffic that had occurred up to 1996 and this represents the first stages of Poland's general move back towards increasing prosperity following the problems of the transition period, a trend also reflected in the other two major Polish ports. Totals for 1996 as a whole year reached 16.3 million tonnes which was an increase over 1995 of about 4% caused largely by increases in grain and coal.

However, the results for iron ore traffic are disappointing. The slow growth in general cargo was welcomed as a trade in which Szczecin had seen severe losses over the previous few years. The data which is not available, from the private wharves and from the ferry activities does indicate some strong growth, particularly in the latter where the combination of Unity Line and PZB's activities are beginning to benefit from the economic improvement of Poland and also from the growth in north-south transit traffic that has occurred following the accession of Sweden and Finland to the European Union - with trade to and from Germany benefiting - and with the growth of the Scandinavian - Middle East markets, including Turkey and Bulgaria in particular.

Figure 26
Szczecin-Świnoujście cargo throughput 1996 (second half year) and 1997 (first half year) (million tonnes)

	COAL	IRON ORE	GENERAL CARGO	TOTAL
1996 (second half year)	3.17	1.70	1.21	7.01
1997 (first half year)	4.22	1.38	1.55	8.10

(NB Totals will not add up as other cargo groups not included - e.g. ferry traffic and private wharves)

Source: Szczecin - Świnoujście Port Authority, 1997

Liner services

Neither Szczecin nor Świnoujście are major liner operating ports as is apparent from the accompanying Figure 27. This is an area that the port would like to develop but which remains problematic as the container facilities available are limited and the competition from Hamburg in particular, is severe.

The most significant of the services provided at present are the regular ferry lines to and from Sweden provided by Unity Line - a collaborative venture of PZM and EuroAfrica - and PZB, operating as the Polish Baltic Shipping Company (Polferries). The latter has recently (summer 1997) changed the service it provides substantially, following the introduction of a new fast catamaran service between Świnoujście and Malmö and soon to include Copenhagen as well. This has replaced a number of conventional ferry services and represents a deliberately competitive policy to match that of Unity Line and its use of the very modern conventional "Polonia" vessel. More of this can be found in earlier chapters on PZM and PZB.

Other services worth noting are those provided by EuroAfrica's conventional general cargo services to West Africa, Finland and Eire, to the UK by Fast Lines from their dedicated terminal noted above, and by Stavangerske Linjefart to and from Norway. Clearly there is considerable potential for further liner developments in both ports as the economy of Poland improves but subject to the severe competitive pressures that the location of Szczecin-Świnoujście as a port suffers in relation to established ports in Germany, the Netherlands and, of course, Gdynia and Gdańsk.

What is also worth noting is the absence of any fully containerised services and the predominance of conventional general cargo facilities. Ro-ro services are clearly important simply through the ferry service provision, although there is also very limited use of the existing ramp in Szczecin by a weekly EuroAfrica service to and from Helsinki and Turku in Finland.

Developments

Szczecin-Świnoujście is not standing still and watching the Polish economy improve without also recognising the need to keep up to date and to compete far more than in the past with other Polish ports, with those in Germany and further west, and with alternative modes in particular, in the form of trucks. As a result, a number of port development proposals have been put forward for consideration and a number of projects are underway or about to be completed. Many of these plans have emerged since the reorganisation of the port in the early 1990s and further developments are now expected to occur as the new 1997 structure and ownership begins to take shape and have an impact. Projects include both upgrading existing facilities and the introduction of new ones.

Figure 27
Szczecin-Świnoujście Liner Services

Destination	Carrier	Type	Frequency
		FROM SZCZECIN	
Cameroon			
Douala	EuroAfrica	Conventional	Bi-monthly
Ivory Coast			
Abidjan	EuroAfrica	Conventional	Monthly
Gambia			
Banjul	EuroAfrica	Conventional	Subject to inducement
Ghana			
Tema	EuroAfrica	Conventional	Monthly
Nigeria			
Lagos	EuroAfrica	Conventional	1-2 monthly
Senegal			
Dakar	EuroAfrica	Conventional	Subject to inducement
Other West African ports	EuroAfrica	Conventional	Subject to inducement
Finland			
Helsinki	EuroAfrica	Ro-ro	Weekly
Turku	EuroAfrica	Ro-ro	Weekly
Ireland			
Dublin	EuroAfrica	Semi-container	Every two weeks

Table 27 continued

UK

Howendyke	Fast Lines	Conventional	4 a month
Perth	Fast Lines	Conventional	monthly
London (Barking)	Fast Lines	Conventional	3 a month
London (Tower Wharf)	Fast Lines	Conventional	3 a month

FROM ŚWINOUJŚCIE

Sweden

Ystad	Unity Line	Rail/truck ferry	2 a day
Ystad	Unity Line	Passenger/rail/ car/truck ferry	1 a day

Denmark

Copenhagen	PZB	Passenger/car ferry	5 a week
Malmö	PZB	High speed catamaran and passenger/car/ truck ferry	2 a day

Source: Szczecin-Świnoušjcie Port Authority, 1997

Many of the plans were outlined in the "Strategic Directions of the Port of Szczecin-Świnoujście Investment Activities" document published in 1992, which accepted the physical division of the port between the two main complexes and that Świnoujście should continue as the main bulk terminal and Szczecin should diversify across a number of fields of activity. Projects include proposals to modernise the existing **container terminal** in Szczecin to facilitate unitised cargo handling of all types and to encourage this trade into the port which is largely absent as a result of the years of state direction of trades, in this case almost exclusively to Gdynia. Current throughput is between 20-30000 TEU per year. This development includes the construction of a modern warehouse, improved road and rail facilities and the extension of the open storage areas. Meanwhile **Chorzowskie Quay** is being modernised and converted from a bulk terminal to one that can handle general cargo including the provision of a ro-ro ramp (the second in Szczecin) and resurfaced hard standing.

The **EWA grain silo facility** has seen new facilities for importing cargo including improved rail links and roads. Storage facilities are also due to be expanded.

The major port improvement that is currently under way is the installation of a **Vessel traffic management System (VTMS)** facility for the channel between Szczecin and Świnoujście, funded from a US$37m World Bank loan negotiated by the state Treasury. Installation of the VTMS should be completed by 1998 and is being constructed by the German company Atlas Elektronic.

The rest of the loan is dedicated towards the improvement of **land based infrastructure** including a series of roads and bridges in the port area and the surrounding region, one of which is a major road based communication across the Odra river. A limited number of rail improvements are also part of the loan. The port authority is quite open in recognising that a third part to the loan is needed to improve the internal communications structure of the port but as yet it has not been forthcoming.

Discussion

Szczecin-Świnoujście Port Authority presents an interesting, if not overly dynamic example of what is occurring in the ports industry of Poland today and the many problems associated with the adaptation of this sector to the new environment in the maritime industry. Despite these problems and the uncertainties of the overall situation, the port was profitable in 1996 and looks set to be in 1997. One major advantage in this process of change that it shares with all the Polish international ports is that the sector in terms of port administration is largely protected from competition from new entrants as within Poland there is very little likelihood that new ports or port facilities will be built in the short term at least. Clearly competition from outside Poland does and has had an effect - typified by the move of traffic to German ports - as does the increasing role of trucks in the distribution industry, taking traditional traffic away from Szczecin-Świnoujście to different routes altogether and the port does show evidence of this pattern with the drop in turnover in the 1990s from which it is now recovering.

Szczecin-Świnoujście also is having to adapt in the structures that it is adopting for the administration and ownership framework within the port with the effects of the new Ports Act coming on stream and the increased private input into the organisation and its operation. Inevitably this will lead to the privatisation of the port authority at some time in the future - along with those in Gdynia and Gdańsk - but this may well be some considerable time away as the need for privatisation within the industry, once the operational side has been successfully transformed, becomes far less urgent. Thus the final stages of separating port and state may be a long way off yet.

The increased involvement of the local city and regional interests are likely to aid this transformation process and will certainly make the port rather more responsive to the local needs. This will be of some considerable importance to the port as the loss of traditional international deep-sea trade through the modal and route changes noted earlier realistically can only be made up from more local traffic.

Bulk traffic remains the clear dominant trade and will inevitably continue to do so as time passes. One problem in this trade however, is that the predominant activity - that relating to coal - is in decline (albeit slowly) and is unlikely to show a major revival as Polish coal increases in cost and industry moves away from such fuels. Oil traffic is minimal by comparison as it is concentrated in Gdańsk and thus without major investment, transfer to this traffic is very unlikely. Ferry traffic is buoyant and increasing and is likely to continue to do so with the accession of Sweden and Finland to the European Union and the eventual accession of Poland sometime over the medium term future. General cargo remains a problem in that Szczecin-Świnoujście has no realistic container facility and the traditional general cargo facilities of the past are now either no longer needed by guaranteed CMEA traffic or have become outdated. Transit traffic from the Czech Republic and Slovakia has also been lost in the changing pattern of trade and transport in Europe.

Szczecin-Świnoujście also has a large number of development plans which match in number the ambitions of those of Gdańsk and Gdynia - and incidentally most of the ports around the Baltic Sea. Particularly notable is the container terminal facility that is planned for a market that is rather more hopeful than apparent at the moment. In addition there is provision for a second ro-ro ramp in Szczecin for services which, at present are non-existent.

The major infrastructural improvement that is currently in progress is that of the Vessel Traffic Management System (VTMS) funded by a World Bank loan. Although highly needed in the context of modern environmental and safety issues, the significance of this development is likely to be less for the region than the land based infrastructure improvements that are also being supported by the World Bank, including road, rail and bridge improvements. Access to both ports needs improving to help regenerate the port's prospects and to relieve the local population of the problems that are known to exist.

Overall, Szczecin-Świnoujście reveals a pattern of adaptation that is widely reflected in all the three major Polish ports and is one driven from the outside and by the state as it pushes forward restructuring and privatisation. In both cases the port industry lags behind that of the shipping sector and even moreso, the ancillary sector, largely because of the nature of its business and the semi competitive framework in which it works. It thus lacks the essential dynamism to develop and adapt in the new economic context and Szczecin-Świnoujście, along with Gdynia and Gdańsk, may find revitalising their ports difficult without some deliberate and definite progress towards a competitive structure. Only then will the initiative be taken by the ports to market themselves effectively in the niches to which they are best adapted or to reframe their objectives in a way that is most in tune with the needs of the Polish and international maritime sector that exist today.

Morska Agencja Gdynia Sp. z.o.o.

Introduction

Morska Agencja Gdynia - otherwise commonly known as MAG - is a company that emerged from the same situation as Morska Agencja Szczecin (MAS) in Szczecin as one of the five divisions of the newly nationalised agency network in Poland established in 1951 and based on the existing private sector network of agencies that had been established prior to the second world war.

The work originally conducted by MAG was to act as the sole, and thus monopolistic, agency for all Polish registered and foreign flagged vessels calling at the Ports of Gdynia, Gdańsk, Darłowo and Ustka and in addition, to represent their owners in Poland. Each agency had its owned specific region and there was no attempt to compete or diversify. Other agencies apart from MAG and MAS existed in the other main industrial centres of Poland but specialised in other modes of transport and as such provided further little competition.

Over the years, under the Communist regime, MAG slowly but surely took on more duties and diversified into other related activities. These focused mainly upon P and I representation and from the early 1980s, crewing, the latter function being a result of pressure from the trades union Solidarność (Solidarity) who wanted regional control of crewing issues rather than one dictated nationally from the centre of government in Warsaw.

Ownership

The ownership situation - i.e. full state control of all assets and all decision-making that goes with this - continued unabated until 1991. MAG was one of the earliest maritime organisations to be affected by ownership changes following the liberalisation phase of the late 1980s. MAG as a private company was established on the 15th October, 1991 and began operating as a fully private organisation on 1st November of the same year. The choice to privatise was undoubtedly a result of the driving ambition of some 15 senior employees of the existing company and the timing of the move a was a result of the existence of extremely favourable leasing terms available in late 1991 - in particular, a considerable reduction in interest rate payments that would be required.

The moves towards privatisation had taken over a year and thus the speed at which the company had moved following liberalisation of the maritime economy was very fast. Privatisation actually took the form of a lease from the state Ministries of Maritime Economy and Privatisation, at a 50% reduction in interest rates over a five year period - i.e. up until December 1996. The new private company owners were required to purchase the company during that time through a series of agreed repayments and satisfactorily finalised the transfer in December of 1996, thus concluding the privatisation process. The state has no ownership claims on the new company, which legally had become subject to the full Polish Commercial Code in November 1991.

Share ownership in the company is restricted to three groups of shareholders - the original senior 15 who represent around 8% of the staff and 30% of the shares; a group of middle managers (25% of staff and 60% of shares); and a substantial number of lesser employees (67% of staff, 10% of shares). As a consequence of this arrangement of ownership, the transfer of MAG was a Management Employee Buyout (MEBO) rather than a co-operative arrangement. It is effectively a private company and not a public one - a deliberate arrangement that fitted the needs of the company and the desires of the majority of shareholders. Private company status results in a greater control of the company by its owners than if public company ownership had been chosen. Capital has always been sufficient for the company's development - albeit sometimes only just. The administration of a private company is also easier, with no Annual General Meeting required for example, although financially there is little difference in Poland from being a public company. The rejection of co-operative status was a reaction to the difficulties presented in allowing full worker involvement and the problems of achieving effective decision-making.

The activities of the company

By late 1997 MAG had increased their diversification of company interests considerably since their days as a state run agency organisation. Agency activities remain the dominant part of the company's work (representing about 15% of the company's income) and MAG is now the biggest agency in Poland. It has offices in all major Polish seaports - this includes Gdynia Port, the Baltic Container Terminal Gdynia, Gdańsk Port and Szczecin Port - and as such has clearly extended its previously constrained spatial role beyond the ports of north-east Poland to those along the entire Baltic Coast. In addition, it has a branch office in Warsaw and overseas offices in London (UK), where MAG Overseas acts as its representative in what they describe as the most important shipping and transport marketplace in the world.

All aspects of international transport are now dealt with at each of the locations and as such this agency work is now only one part of the company's interests - albeit the biggest part. Crewing agency work has remained a significant activity since it was introduced in 1980 - some 10% of income - the company specialising in the supply of qualified Polish seagoing personnel for all kinds of foreign registered and owned vessels including complete crews or single seaman, both officers and ratings. Crews are supplied all over the world, although the majority are to be found with USA and European shipowners. One example from the UK is Crescent Shipping, which takes over 100 personnel, representing 95% of their crews. MAG claims to be the biggest crewing agency in Poland and thus one of the biggest in the world. Liner representation is also an important company feature (around 12% of income), providing the facilities for intermodal and co-ordinated freight transport, both containerised and conventional, and P and I Club representation which includes acting as correspondents in the process of claims handling and the protection of the owners' interests. Examples of P and I Club retention includes the United Kingdom based West of England and Liverpool clubs and Skuld from Norway.

These activities, which to a large extent were inherited from the existing state company, have now been joined by freight forwarding (10% of income), including shipping project cargo, heavy lift and conventional shipments, ship chartering, broking and a variety of related financial services. In the mid 1990s, MAG has now also quietly become involved in conducting international trade as importers of coal into Poland - in contrast to the large quantity of exports of coal that are normally the case. The price structure of the coal sector has attracted MAG to this activity as a sideline to its normal business interests. Understandably it is a politically sensitive area in which to become involved but whilst profitable, the new climate within the Polish maritime sector makes it both of interest and acceptable (just).

Two further minor activities have also been incorporated into the company's portfolio in the mid 1990s - these are fishing equipment supply and the development of real estate, the latter including an area of land adjacent to the new motorway near Gdańsk and also a development of warehousing and industrial units behind the company's newly refurbished offices in Gdynia. Both these latter two activities - fishing equipment supply and real estate development - are conducted through subsidiary companies in which MAG has a shareholding which varies between 40 and 60%.

The diversification noted above provides a safety net for the company if one market should decline severely and reflects expansion either into related fields (e.g. forwarding), where money can be made (e.g. real estate), or both (e.g. coal). Reflecting the company's desire for professionalism in its work, it is a member of both BIMCO and the Polish Shipbroking Association. This latter organisation is now the fee setting group for agency and broking work in Poland, a function it has taken up to replace the role of the state in this sector. Membership and rate compliance are both voluntary.

Company structure

MAG has followed a very deliberate simple framework in the development of company structure following privatisation. At the head of the company is a Supervisory Board which provides guidance to the Executive Board below them who are responsible for the day to day running of the company as a whole. Beneath the Executive Board are a series of departments with specific responsibilities including crewing, forwarding, agency work, P and I representation etc.. Subsidiary companies involved in real estate and fish equipment supply have representatives on their boards varying in proportion to the ownership stake that MAG has.

All the departments are claimed to be operationally free which facilitates decision-making and encourages flexibility. The main exception to this is the Finance Department which is both highly centralised and heavily controlled. In the climate of financial risk and uncertainty of the new Poland this was felt to be necessary.

Marketing was not concentrated within one department but in true modern Polish style, was spread across all departments each maintaining their own links - begging questions of co-ordination, co-operation, duplication and strategy. The corporate image of the company was defined for example, by advertisements and brochures which followed the same pattern of presentation, design, colours and logo. However, although a subjective issue, there is little doubt that the image chosen is both dull and uninspiring, awaiting a western lift.

Immediately prior to privatisation, the company employed around 254 persons, a decline from around 390 in 1988. By the time of purchase in late 1991, this had already fallen to 198 and by late 1997 was down to 182 despite the increased range of activities and the new geographical spread to Szczecin and Warsaw. Some 50% of all these employees had worked with MAG for 15 to 20 years implying great stability in the workforce - but also increasing age and thus potentially a problem with new ideas and initiatives.

Competition

Only five real competitors exist for MAG as an agency company in the Gdynia/Gdańsk area, although, of course, with the range of activities that has now been taken on by the company, the opportunities for meeting competition are now that much greater. Apart from these five competitor agencies, there are probably another 20-30 operating within Gdynia/Gdańsk but who are small and relatively unimportant. It is estimated that MAG is responsible, post privatisation, for around 50% of the Gdynia/Gdańsk agency work. Major competitors to MAG include Polfracht, Aksmarine, Uni-Consult, PUBC, Marbalco, the PZM tanker agency subsidiary and Okmarit, the latter set up by ex MAG employees.

MAG's deliberate plan is to offer a wide range of services so that all the needs of the industry can be met in-house or through a subsidiary company, thus differentiating themselves from their immediate agency competitors. This fits in well with the desire to protect themselves by diversifying against the downward trends that occur within all marketplaces on occasions.

The establishment of the Szczecin office is a good example of how MAG has diversified within a core activity and the new office will pass demands from clients in Szczecin that they cannot meet, to their headquarters in Gdynia where the diversification of functions is much greater.

The Szczecin office contrasts markedly with the entrenched, narrow outlook of former partners in the agency market in state owned days - for example, MAS who as we shall see in a later chapter, has remained largely faithful to its inherited area and functions. Prior to establishing the new office, MAG used sub-agents but found that there was a considerable degree of customer dissatisfaction with this arrangement. Local reaction in Szczecin was somewhat varied with the port advising them against expansion as there were over 20 agents already, and MAS irritated by the arrival of a previous partner to compete with them. MAG has done well so far and by late 1997 was handling over 200 ships a year - although this needs to be placed besides the Gdynia/Gdańsk number of over 1800. Incidentally, this represents a decline from around 3400 vessels in 1988 of which some 22% were Polish flagged.

Discussion

MAG is a highly successful, fully privatised maritime company in Poland and represents one of the major achievements in this sector since the transition of the late 1980s. It is profitable - and has been since its transformation - and turnover has multiplied six-fold since its monopoly was lost and the process of extensive diversification has taken place. Even though some of this growth in turnover has been due to currency fluctuations, the results nevertheless remain impressive particularly in comparison with some other enterprises in the maritime sector where financial problems have dominated.

The company is successful because of its determination to diversify and its recognition of the need to spread beyond its inherited spatial influence and its existing market base. It thus has actively entered the market with a range of ancillary maritime services, not only in the Gdańsk/Gdynia area but also in its main rival marketplace of Szczecin, where it now competes openly and actively with its companion of old times MAS - the latter notably constrained to old markets and locations. Diversification is the key to success that we have seen throughout the Polish maritime scene and neglect of this fundamental principle of western economies can be seriously important for the emerging ex-state maritime sector.

Early privatisation in comparison with much of the sector in Poland has also helped and MAG was assisted here by the discounted interest rates available from the state and the fact that it was emerging from a largely non-political branch of the industry where it was relatively uncontentious to enter the private sector. This contrasts markedly with the tardiness of privatisation moves in the ports sector and the problems of the three state shipping companies that continue to dog their progression. MAG is now fully privatised, liberated from the controls that the state retains over many companies and free to develop as they wish. The result has been a series of profitable years, a thriving company client portfolio and an increasing range of interests to carry the company through bad times in their core agency work. The method of privatisation chosen has also helped in the subsequent development of the company as it restricts decision-making to relatively few people and facilitates a close control upon the activities and progress of the company as it moves into new markets. The rather more 'democratic' privatisation processes of share sales and widespread employee co-operatives, have been studiously avoided.

There is some way still to go and MAG does face serious competition in all the areas in which it works. The marketing structures within the company remain questionable and will need revising from the traditional approach utilising personal contacts and reliance upon individuals within the various branches of the company. This should manifest itself through a more dynamic physical presence in time - matching that of the company's headquarters in Gdynia which to all intents and purposes is a modern western company office.

Overall, MAG presents an interesting example of the most progressive of ancillary companies in the new Polish maritime environment and an example of at least one way in which a state owned enterprise can progress reasonably quickly into one with many western characteristics and as such, within the relatively conservative and stagnant market place of the traditional agency sector, can develop and survive. MAG represents an example of a company that has emerged from state ownership to provide serious competition in a sector where new, small private companies are rapidly eating away at traditional markets and as such, has the opportunity to avoid capitulation to these new private competitors - but it has achieved this not through relying on their old markets and any remains of a privileged status, but through adopting a modern and western approach to the needs of the industry and the way that companies in Poland in the future will need to progress and develop. It will be an interesting period coming up as MAG continues to adapt and most probably, moves into further new business areas as the opportunities arise. The contrast with their immediate competitors will be similarly interesting.

Morska Agencja Szczecin Limited

Introduction

Morska Agencja Szczecin (MAS) is now a multi-functional port agency related organisation also offering a variety of services including average adjusting, shipbroking and crew supplies from their headquarters in Szczecin. MAS originated from the state owned monopolistic regime of the old system in a structure that resembled that of many other parts of the maritime sector including C. Hartwig, Polfracht and Baltona as well as the strictly defined shipping and ports industries.

Both MAS and Morska Agencja Gdynia (MAG) began operations in 1951 under the new Communist state government originating from the range of existing private sector agency companies that had dominated in Poland during the 1930s and immediately after the end of the war. A number of agency companies existed then, many with western capital backing including finance from Sweden and Denmark. MAS inherited this structure in 1951 with responsibility for agency services in the major ports of Szczecin, Świnoujście and Kołobrzeg and also in the minor locations of Police, Stepnica and Gryf. MAG was constrained to the Gdynia/Gdańsk area. No competition in providing agency services was permitted and both MAG and MAS kept strictly to their respective geographical locations. Both co-operated with each other when circumstances dictated that their businesses should overlap.

Ownership and company structure

Following the political and economic changes of 1989, the monopoly provisions were removed and competition over geographical area and from a newly emerging private sector was permitted. Unlike the shipping sector, where the capital needed to invest in the market is very high and, as a consequence, competition is constrained even when the political and economic environment is liberalised, the agency sector requires very little investment and success depends mainly upon the knowledge, experience and contacts of the individuals concerned. Thus a new competitor can set up with little more than a small office, telephone and fax machine and less essentially yet in Poland, a computer. The result in MAS's market was an immediate proliferation of competitors looking to take a small piece of the Szczecin port and shipping agency market, commonly ex-state employees and frequently ex-MAS employees. Many would serve only one ship a month but in aggregate they form a formidable competitive environment for MAS in the region.

The competition had existed to a very limited extent at the end of the 1980s with the first liberalisation of the Polish economy under the old regime but the real developments did not begin to occur until 1989. Since then the market has become almost entirely privatised and freed from many of the constraints formally imposed by the Communist government.

MAS was privatised in 1993 following the government decree of the previous year that permitted the privatisation of such organisations. It is now a fully fledged limited company owned entirely by a combination of the current employees and a number of ex-workers who have now retired. All potential investors had to purchase shares in the company - none were available free, unlike some other privatisation initiatives - at a price pre-determined by the state which was supposed to reflect the company's value. Initially, 20% of the value of the company was sold off to the employees whilst the remaining 80% was retained by the state to be paid for slowly over an agreed five year period to be completed at the end of 1998. This loan from the state is charged interest at a preferential rate, less than the commercial rate, and upon the final payment the shareholders become owners of the company. However, full privatised status is granted upon the payment of the initial 20% stake with all the benefits relating to flexibility, finance and freedom of action that this brings.

The 20% employee share was difficult to find in the case of MAS and a substantial number of employees could not afford to take part in the privatisation process. The shares are now tradable but only between the existing owners - eventually, the long term plan is to allow sale to employees who are non-shareholders and then at an even later date to anyone who should wish to invest in the company. However, no dates have been set for the final completion of this process. Further progress awaits loan completion, legal moves and agreement in the courts with the state Treasury. Strict laws govern all these procedures and all decisions require the approval of the existing shareholders.

The resulting structure of the company that has emerged as a result of the privatisation and liberalisation process is fairly unclear. At the head of the company is a Board of Directors elected by the shareholders at the Annual General Meeting and which tends to be dominated by a narrow collection of individuals who possess a large proportion of the shares of MAS. Underneath the Board is the Council, which is a requirement of the commercial legislation of Poland for limited companies, and which consists of a number of MAS employees plus an unspecified number of outsiders - in late 1997 they numbered only one who was a representative of the Port of Szczecin-Świnoujście. Others who might have appeared on the council include representatives of the companies that MAS deals with. The total Council size was five in late 1997 but could vary in time. Each member is voted in (or out) by the Board of Directors who also sets their salary. The main function of the Council is to monitor the work of the Board in directing the company and also in appointing on behalf of the Board, the senior managers. Below the level of the Council are the working members of staff of MAS.

These staff members are split into four different working groups. The agency department providing ship and port agency facilities for the ports of Szczecin, Świnoujście and Kołobrzeg, plus local ports like Stepnica and Police; the averaging department provides services relating to average adjusting and ship repairs; the service department provides for vessel needs including crewing, stores and bunkering; and the accounts department provides financial and administrative back-up. There is also an internal related company - Polbroker - based in the same Szczecin location - which provides full shipbroking and chartering services but for the ports of Darłowo and Ustka as well. This range of functions represents a considerable increase on the narrow set that were the responsibility of the old MAS but notably remains constrained to highly related activities and does not reflect a true sprit of diversification.

Employee numbers have dropped considerably since privatisation from a peak in the mid 1980s of around 130 when MAS was the monopoly agency suppliers of the region, to a level of only 36 in 1997 - 30 based at the Szczecin headquarters, three at Kołobrzeg port and three at Świnoujście port. This is despite the increase in range of activities and is a reflection of the effects of privatisation and the result of competition.

In addition, privatisation has also brought substantial rises in rent for their headquarters building and active consideration is being given to plans to move elsewhere to reduce costs. A reduction in the space rented has already occurred.

Competition and trades

As noted earlier, a large number of competitor agency providers soon developed in the Szczecin region once the state controls had been removed in 1989. By 1997, it was estimated that some 40 or more competitors existed in Szczecin alone plus a number of others in Świnoujście [1], Police [1], Ustka [1], Darłowo [1], Kołobrzeg [1], Gryf [1] and Trzebiez [1]. The very large majority of these new companies have been formed by ex-employees of MAS who have taken their experience and contacts from the former state company and used this as the basis for establishing their own sole trade, activities free from even the few legal constraints that exist for private limited companies such as MAS. In a curious way this has helped MAS a little in coping with its employment difficulties in that it provided a means of reducing staffing levels at a time when forced redundancies may have been politically and certainly socially difficult. It has however, raised the level of competition to a severe level with clear impact upon MAS itself.

Many of the new competitors have attracted, albeit small quantities of investment from overseas - particularly Denmark and Sweden, reflecting the close contacts of this part of Poland to these regions maintained through the local ferry routes to Malmö, Copenhagen and Ystad. Curiously it also repeats the spatial investment pattern of the pre war years in the Szczecin region and the port agency sector. This overseas investment enables these new small competitors to pay high wages to their limited number of employees and to provide a high level of technology and service to their clients causing MAS further problems. This reflects trends elsewhere in the maritime sector - e.g. the development of POL Levant as a response to the state constraints upon conditions and pay within Polish Ocean Lines. MAS claim that they have rationalised their own activities so much that their "pay and conditions is (sic) almost indistinguishable from those of the private sector."

One cause of all this rationalisation at MAS and an effect of the growth of competition has been the decline in turnover at MAS. During the mid 1980s when MAS was a state monopoly, some 3000 vessels a year were regularly served. This has now reduced to between 1200 and 1300 with consequent effects upon the staffing levels and the financial status of the company. An indication of the changes in client is the loss of the very sizeable PZM market over recent years as PZM have developed their own chartering and agency activities. Now, PZM work is rare and usually emerges when PZM's client insists on using MAS. It remains the largest agency in Szczecin by far and has no vessel type specialisation, acting for all those who request its services, of any trade within the region. Port traffic is reasonably diverse but dominated by Szczecin and Świnoujście based commodities such as coal, iron ore, grain and chemical fertilisers. A little general cargo is also served. Transit traffic remains important but less so than in the days before the economic changes. It is currently dominated by the Czech Republic, Austria, Hungary and Slovakia. However, some losses are clearly significant including, for example that of the old Czech Ocean Shipping Company - the once Czechoslovakian state ocean-going ship operator, whose base was Szczecin but whose successor is now based in Hamburg. Detailed information upon levels of profit in recent years is not available and further data about the company's activities were not retained as "it (sic) is not needed". Profits have always been achieved since privatisation, and the reduction in bureaucracy stemming from the company's structural changes, have helped considerably in maintaining the financial viability of MAS.

The issue of marketing is largely ignored, relying on the contacts that the company has made over the previous 47 years of existence and thus concentrating upon a hard core of traditional customers who have remained loyal during the changing phases of agency work in Poland. There have been no attempts to establish a wider customer base although, as we saw earlier, there have been attempts to move into a number of diversified, if related, service areas such as P and I work and that of broking. A conscious decision has been made not to become involved formally with overseas or foreign companies as MAS sees no need to move beyond its established contacts around the world.

Meanwhile, their sub-agency work is quite active; MAS acts as sub-agents for a large number of companies in the Szczecin region and also commonly sub-contracts work outside the area, particularly in the Gdynia/Gdańsk region, as and when necessary. No thought had been given to the idea of establishing a regional office in the latter despite the changes in the structure of the industry and the invasion of the Szczecin and Świnoujście ports by their old partner Morska Agencja Gdynia (MAG).

We have seen already that MAS has shown little, if any interest in diversifying the activities of the company in terms of the geographical area served and that other companies, and in particular MAG has entered the Szczecin regional market to compete with them. In terms of functions, MAS has shown a little more interest and now advertises itself as involved in chartering and P and I business for example. However, the quantity of such business is strictly limited and represents a very small proportion of its activities. In the words of the company they "have no knowledge of other sectors and no experience" and hence no plans to develop this side of the company especially whilst the agency activities are profitable.

One particularly fierce area of competition stems from the port tariff basis for the agency services provided in Poland (62). MAS is a significant member of the Polish Shipbrokers Association which is responsible for the setting of agreed tariffs between the members of the group which includes all the significant players in both the Gdynia/Gdańsk and the Szczecin/Świnoujście markets. Agreed agency fees are published by the Association and are supposedly non-negotiable but it appears that they are frequently adjusted (downwards) particularly for valued customers and by the new, smaller, private agencies who thus capture traffic they otherwise would not have had. Some evidence of effective "dumping" prices by new agencies also exists, to gain a place in the market at the early stages of their development. Thus competition can be fierce despite the existence of a cartel of pricing - whose continued existence can be questioned as a result of the need to adapt to meet European Union demands - which has been developed from the Communist regime days, to support and protect the industry members.

Discussion

This brief analysis of the activities of MAS indicates a number of interesting areas for discussion that, in some ways, typify the development of the Polish maritime sector during the transition years of the 1990s. These issues can be summarised through discussion of one particular set of characteristics of the company.

There is an obvious and clear failure of the company to develop the practices and attitudes needed to thrive, or even survive in the current maritime marketplace. Despite the success of privatisation of the company, there is no indication that this has had any real marked impact upon MAS which continues to rely on what is left of its current client base and which has failed to take any realistic steps to diversify its market either in terms of clients or in terms of its location or activities. It is not that it is unaware of the spread of diversification within the industry and it is quite open about the existence and success of MAG from Gdynia, for example, invading its geographical territory and reducing its own client base - it is just that there has been no response to it and no attempt to set up a MAS operation in the Gdańsk/Gdynia area. The same is largely true of the type of work that is undertaken which remains very largely dominated by the activities in port and ships agency that it had undertaken before the political, social and economic changes of the late 1980s and the early 1990s.

This inactivity is possibly a result of the staffing problems that have been faced in recent years as the company has had to lose a large number of employees and that the majority who have left have not only been the young and dynamic but also have gone on to set up their own companies in direct competition to MAS or have joined the newly developing activities of other existing competitors such as MAG, Polsteam Agencies and so on. What is left is an ageing employment base with little incentive to develop and be innovative in the way they approach the market - a problem that we have noted before, for example in the rump of Polish Ocean Lines in Gdynia. It may be that this employment restructuring process that is going on in the ex-state companies is an inevitable consequence of the changes within the sector and that it reflects the privatisation and reorganisation phases that are being experienced at the moment. With time, MAS and others who have failed to react sufficiently and adequately to the new situation may well disappear from the market place, consumed by the new multifunctional organisations that have either adapted to the new needs of their client base, or emerged as new private sector companies rather more aware of the developing situation in the maritime ancillaries market.

This rather depressing picture was also reflected in the lack of detail available from the financial and statistical point of view and perhaps more significantly, from the attitudes expressed towards the need for such information and the uses to which it can be put. One of the most notable characteristics of the modern Polish maritime sector is its use and desire for more information and its awareness of the need for detailed and accurate financial and trade statistics and trends. No indication of this came from MAS who were happy to rely upon their knowledge of the market as it once existed and to confine itself to the client base it once had and the sectors with which it was experienced and comfortable.

There remains the possibility that MAS will develop, adapt and survive in the new environment and in so doing may find that it too can diversify spatially and into new clients and market sectors. However, this process may have to wait for the changes in the company management that inevitably will take place over the coming years as the senior employees reach the age of retirement. It will be particularly interesting then to examine the changing styles in management that may (or may not) emerge and whether these changes will be adequate to stimulate MAS and lead to its progressive development within the maritime sector of Szczecin and beyond. Other companies in a similar position - and here we can include Polish Ocean Lines and a number of the subsidiaries - have now progressed from their position as state departments and entered the new environment with all the adaptations that requires. Polska Żegluga Bałtycka (PZB) for example, who we examined in an earlier chapter, has shown late signs of entering the privatised world and taking on board the new attitudes and approaches needed. It remains to be seen if MAS can do the same.

Polfracht Shipbroking and Chartering

Introduction

Polfracht Shipbroking and Chartering Co. dates from its formation in 1951 as the state owned monopoly provider of broking and chartering services in Poland and from then until 1957 it was responsible for all Polish activities in this sector. A change in law enabled very limited competition to develop from that date but in most respects the monopoly remained. It remains based in its original location in Gdynia from which it has continued to serve the Polish marketplace in all ports. It originated from two companies who had been operating in this sector from the 1930s and was formed by the newly constituted Communist government after the second world war to provide services to the Polish fleet, importers and exporters. As we shall see later in this section, Polfracht once had the complete monopoly of broking and chartering activities in Poland on behalf of the extensive network of Foreign Trade Organisations (FTO) who were the state bodies responsible for the organisation of all exports and imports to and from Poland and through whom under the old system all international trade had to pass by law, had to be conducted and for all sectors of Polish shipping. However, it is worth noting here that even under the old system, Polfracht handled all its business on a commercial basis with due respect for the practices and rates prevailing on international freight markets.

In fact most of the work undertaken up until the late 1980s was on behalf of Polska Żegluga Morska (PZM) and Polska Żegluga Bałtycka (PZB). Most of the activity relating to Polskie Linie Oceanicze (POL) in the liner sector was undertaken by the shipping company itself for reasons that seem to be lost in the mists of time. Polfracht, in the late 1980s had developed a world-wide agency and representative system to sustain this domination and to provide adequate standards of service for their two major clients. This monopolistic situation did not allow or encourage diversification and clearly did not focus the company's mind upon competition nor quality of service.

The company

Polfracht remains a major broker in the Polish maritime market place despite the massive changes that have taken place. Ownership remains 100% by the state although the relationship between state and company has changed substantially. Interference from the Ministry is now rare as long as the company continues to make profits and is effectively one meeting a year with state officials in Warsaw. There is no direct influence on what the company does on a day to day basis including employment levels and pay agreements. There is no direct subsidy paid to the company by the state and all normal company taxes are paid in full as with any other state owned company today. It should be emphasised that all profits remain with the company to decide to reinvest, increase salaries, increase staff etc. after tax has been paid.

One major change taking place in 1996 was a change in ownership by the state as in November of that year there was a substantial revision of ministerial functions with a newly expanded and sizeable Treasury taking over the broad strategic responsibility for the maritime sector (including Polfracht) but relinquishing some day to day activities to more local political bodies. As a result, the regional government of Gdańsk will now have direct responsibility for the company until any privatisation proposals become both acceptable and established.

True competition entered Polfracht's protected and established market from 1989 onwards so that by 1996 there were 10 major companies in the broking sector and an increasing number of very small companies commonly consisting of a single individual. From this date as well, all Polfracht's broking and chartering activities have been conducted on an identical basis to the west and every shipping company or shipper can enter into negotiations with a foreign company and vice versa. Polfracht itself has around 42 employees in total with some 20 of these being day to day brokers. Two persons are employed solely on the marketing side of the company, two form the senior management (managing director and his deputy) and the remainder are a variety of receptionists and administrators. These staffing numbers have been gradually reduced from since the early 1990s but no more reductions are anticipated at the moment.

Polfracht remains by far the biggest of all the broking companies in Poland claiming to arrange around 85-90% of all fixtures for Polish and foreign market vessels in Poland outside of the POL and PZM sectors. Thus Polfracht estimate that they have lost only around 10-15% of their previous monopoly of broking for Poland (excluding POL and PZM). In 1995, Polfracht fixed approximately 1000 vessels and almost 10 million tons of cargo. However, some significant competition does exist even with this sizeable market share. The main competitor is Polsteam Brokers formed from the Polska Żegluga Morska group in 1991 to fix PZM's own ships and thus reduce internal costs. Although Polsteam Brokers do conduct work on the wider market, 99% of their work is for PZM from which they make a very substantial profit. The potential for competition does exist as a result albeit one not fully realised at the moment. The remaining competition in Polish broking consists of the very small companies noted above almost all of which are populated by ex Polfracht personnel. In fact some 80-90% of Polsteam Broker's employees are also ex Polfracht.

The structure within which the company now has to operate, following central government reorganisation, is shown in Figure 28. Figure 29 gives details of the functional structure showing the diversity of commodities dealt with and the internal management of the company.

Figure 28
Polfracht Shipbroking and Chartering company organisation

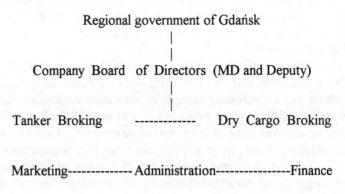

Regional government of Gdańsk

Company Board of Directors (MD and Deputy)

Tanker Broking -------------- Dry Cargo Broking

Marketing-------------- Administration-----------------Finance

Source: Author

One of the first effects of the social, political and economic changes that took place in Poland at the end of the 1980s upon Polfracht was that the company was allowed to diversify and recognising the likelihood of increased competition in the broking sector the company turned to other activities of which the major one today forms a substantial "daughter" company. Polfracht

Shipping Agency is also based in the same building in Gdynia and was formed in 1990 to provide agency services to the shipping industry as a whole in all ports of Poland. It has offices in all the major ports of Gdańsk, Gdynia and Szczecin and is run on entirely independent lines. In 1995 it serviced some 700+ ships and as such ranks as the second biggest agency in Poland (after MAG). It contributed in 1995, some 28-30% of the income of Polfracht as a whole and as such represents an important asset of the company.

In addition to this major diversification, Polfracht has also set up a ship management company which is currently left dormant awaiting the best commercial moment to start trading.

Under the rather curious rules laid down in Polish company law, Polfracht Shipping Agency is deemed to be a private limited company even though it is 100% owned by Polfracht Shipbroking which as we noted earlier, remains a wholly state owned organisation. As a private limited company Polfracht Shipping Agency has a Board of Directors but no Workers Council, unlike Polfracht Shipbroking which does and must take account of the opinions of that Council. Workers Councils can block all strategic decisions in a state owned company and clearly possess considerable power. In those companies which are constituted as private companies, managerial flexibility is notably increased. Polfracht Shipbroking was very keen to emphasise that there were no problems with Workers Councils in their company due to the small nature of the organisation - it is in fact only in the sizeable, old and heavy industrial sectors (e.g. shipbuilding) where real managerial problems with Workers Councils exist. Taxation levels are almost the same in both companies despite the differences in ownership. Income is taxed 40% in both cases but Polfracht Shipping Agency is taxed 0% on profits, Polfracht Shipbroking is taxed 15%, a situation that has existed since 1st January, 1996. This provides a small incentive to form private companies something which Polfracht has considered for some time now and upon which the employees are very keen. However, despite a number of attempts it is proving to be a very long, slow and tortuous political process. In August 1992 Polfracht was on the verge of full privatisation, undertaking detailed talks with the Treasury and employing a series of consultants to look at ways of placing the company in the private sector. Plans centred around selling the company to the existing employees and the major difficulty at that time was agreeing a value for the company and its complex set of joint ventures in which it had a number of interests. These included Gdynia-America Line in New York and London, POL-Hansa in Hamburg and POL-Ascomarit in Genoa (all part of the Polskie Linie Oceanicze combine). Shareholdings of around 15-20% also exist in a number of representative offices world-wide. All joint venture activities are private joint stock companies and thus benefit from the lower tax regime and simplification of management structures.

Figure 29
Internal structure. Polfracht 1996.

Managing Directors (2)

Senior Tanker Chartering Manager

Senior Dry Cargo Chartering Manager

Divisions :-
Minerals, Fertilisers
Coals, Ores, Steel Products, Scrap
Grains, Seeds, Derivatives
Crude Oils, Oil Products, Vegetable Oils
Perishable Cargoes, Refrigerated
Forwarding Logistics
Marketing
Small/Medium Bulk Carriers
Handy/Panamax Bulk Carriers
Multipurpose, Roro, Container
Post Fixture/Documentation
Legal Advice
S&P, Ship Repair Contracting, Sea Towage
Port Agency - Gdynia
Port Agency - Gdańsk
Port Agency - Szczecin

Source : Polfracht Shipbroking and Chartering, Gdynia, Poland.

Unlike most privatisations the plan was that the entire company would be sold to the employees (then numbering around 85), possibly because the company was relatively small compared with some of the larger state owned enterprises. However, despite all the promising noises still nothing had been finalised by late 1997. The preference by then was still for a total employee buyout and preferably before any form of compulsory privatisation was suggested so that the prospective buyers could design and control the process as they wished.

One other major asset that Polfracht possesses is the building in which it is located in Gdynia. Constructed in 1971 and thus relatively modern, Polfracht still administers the building but now occupies only the top two floors for all its activities. The rest is sublet to a variety of differing organisations thus creating a profitable source of regular income. Meanwhile, Polfracht themselves have invested heavily in high-tech equipment within the offices and the most advanced communications facilities, partly because it helps to make them more efficient in day to day business but also because it helps to reduce profits and thus saves on tax.

Prior to 1990 there was no attempt to market the brokering services of Polfracht as there was no need in a monopolistic environment. Although the competition that has developed in the last few years remains comparatively small, there exists now a need to be aware of other players in the market and to adopt an active marketing strategy to ensure market position. The company for many years has conducted market research but the attitude has now expanded so that the brokers that travel widely as part of their broker client services, are also expected to market actively the company at the same time. Meanwhile, a separate department (of two persons) has been created to market the company and from this has developed such clear promotional activities as the development of the new logo which is entirely different from the traditional shipping logos adopted by the state and subsequently retained by PZM, POL, ZPSA and others.

Limited advertising is also used in the trade press both in Poland and abroad particularly associated with special reports on the maritime sector - for example in Fairplay, Lloyds List or Lloyd's Ship Manager. In addition, regular monthly reports on the state of the market are sent free to regular and established clients and at cost to others on demand. Occasional special reports - for example on coal, iron ore or grain trades - are also published in competition from the western specialists such as Drewry's and SSY. Copies of all these publications are sent to all relevant Ministries in central government, to the regional authorities and to a selection of weekly and daily newspapers.

Direct marketing to new sources of trade is normally confined to freight sources, rather than the shipping companies and is highly restricted anyway. Consultancy work, for a fee, has expanded considerably and includes pre-contractual advice. Occasionally this is made available free to the larger principals.

One of the more interesting and perhaps surprising effects of the new commercial market in Poland has been the emergence of a multitude of new products and thus manufacturers who have little or no knowledge of the transport sector and its organisation. Polfracht aims to win a good proportion of these new market players by convincing them of their experience and these new companies' needs of a transport partner. Many of the old Foreign Trade Organisations (FTOs) are now successful privatised exporters and dealers in their old fields of trade and need a broking partner to help them along.

Polfracht's long term association with these organisations has helped it to dominate this area of market growth.

In terms of current client split, Polfracht's main dealings are with Polish industry commonly through the ex FTOs, and in particular in the fields of steel mills and other commercial products. All of the PZM trade, once the biggest part of Polfracht's market, has been lost to Polsteam Brokers, and of course, POL have since 1957 controlled their own markets. Polska Żegluga Bałtycka (PZB) the ferry operator, remains a reasonably important client. The remainder of clients, estimated at around 35% of activity, are foreign ship fixtures. This latter market is characterised by Soviet vessels who represent nearly half of all foreign vessels fixed and whose local port of call is normally Hamburg and sometimes Copenhagen. Only German foreign fixtures exceed this Soviet number.

Polfracht continues to play an active part in the committee work of BIMCO and a variety of other international regulatory bodies. It is also a member of the Polish Shipbroking Association.

Discussion

A number of issues emerge from the details given above in relation to Polfracht and its role in the new Polish business environment.

Firstly, the success of Polfracht in surviving the change from a monopolistic, uncompetitive market environment to one where new competing companies are entering the market and taking business away is partly at least down to the business-like principles upon which the company has been based for many years and the good relations that have developed as a result. Indeed Polfracht is the only state owned broking and chartering organisation of the old east Europe to have survived the changes - and every CMEA country had an enterprise of this sort. The move into the truly commercial sector has been eased as a result with the loss of only a relatively small proportion of business through mainly, the diversification of the PZM group into the broking and chartering sector.

Secondly, Polfracht has in fact continued to dominate the market in Poland for broking and chartering largely based upon the connections within the business that it has continued to maintain. The level of inertia within the industry, combined with trust of the existing and incumbent player has encouraged this market retention. New entrants have much to prove before they are trusted, exemplified by Polsteam Brokers who although successful, have attracted only limited business outside that of PZM, their parent owner.

Thirdly, the competition as a result, has remained very fragmented consisting of a reasonably large number of very small companies, commonly populated by ex-Polfracht employees. Market domination for Polfracht will help it to continue to dominate amongst the 50 or so brokers and charterers that currently exist including well known established companies (in other sectors) such as Morska Ajencja Szczecin, Polsteam and various ship operators who have attempted to diversify into this field.

Fourthly, in terms of diversification, Polfracht has also moved beyond its original area of expertise in the development of the agency arm and its sizeable success. Plans also exist for movement into the ship management business when the time is right reflecting the noticeable trend within the maritime sector as a whole towards increasing the range of activities and services available and offered to the maritime community - in turn helping to ensure financial viability and security. In this case, the risk is limited as it involves minimal investment unlike other companies (e.g. PZM and its involvement in property and land).

Fifthly, it has been particularly disappointing to Polfracht itself that there has been so little progress towards privatisation. Complicated by the relationships between Polfracht and its joint venture companies and confused by a complex set of political agendas that have interrupted the process, almost nothing tangible has been achieved. The company employees remain committed to the process and as far as can be assessed, the state owners are similarly concerned with the need to transfer the company for the benefit of growth and employee incentive. Despite this failure, Polfracht has changed image (unlike most Polish state owned maritime enterprises) and appears to be progressive and profitable. Its prospects in the private sector would be extremely good based on a long tradition of good business practice and a large and faithful customer base. It seems unlikely that before long the move will be made. This progressive nature reveals itself in the slimmed down version of the company, the style of the office location, the explicit recognition of business principles applied to tax avoidance and the impressive technical qualities that have resulted.

Finally, it will be interesting to see how the new ownership structure affects all these issues and the process of privatisation in particular. It may be the case that the new regional government owners will encourage the sale at the earliest possible time, unfettered by the historical baggage of the ministry. There again, it may be that they will view Polfracht as a profitable organisation that should be retained for its income into regional coffers.

Overall it represents an interesting ancillary organisation that is in the throes of moving away from the state - or trying to - and the next few years up to the turn of the century, should prove interesting ones in the life of this company.

C. Hartwig Gdynia

Introduction

C. Hartwig of Gdynia emerged from the state owned group of Hartwig companies that had been established in the early 1950s and which, in turn, was a descendant of the private sector Hartwig group that first saw life in the 1850s. As also noted in the later chapter covering the activities of Hartwig in Szczecin, the group had been divided into five operating companies - three for sea based freight forwarding at Gdynia, Gdańsk and Szczecin, and two for other modes at Warsaw (specialising in air, truck and some rail) and Katowice (specialising in rail and some truck). In respect of the sea based companies, each developed specialisms related to their local markets with, for example, Szczecin concentrating upon bulk shipments and Gdynia more upon container and general cargo movements and in markets in North America and the Far East reflecting local Polish Ocean Line services.

Privatisation

In similar fashion to all other maritime related enterprises, Hartwig Gdynia remained under state ownership and control throughout the post-war period, although it revealed a level of initiative and independence far in excess of other companies of the time when in 1974, they moved into the US market establishing a joint venture with a US freight forwarding company, in setting up Amerpol in the USA. In 1991, Hartwig bought out their US partner and since then has had full control of the operation.

In 1976, the group Hartwig was split formally into five operating companies, legally separate in all ways, although all still state owned and this in itself was a fairly dramatic step forward in reducing state influence over the market and beginning to introduce a spirit of competition. However, little else on this front occurred until the 1989/1990 period when the Polish maritime sector was deregulated and the formal monopoly of Hartwig removed allowing competitors from other existing and new companies to come in and practise. Any remaining semblance of geographical or modal monopoly disappeared very quickly and the Hartwig companies, including that of Gdynia found themselves exposed to the full force of competition (65).

The response by two of the companies in the group - Gdynia and Gdańsk - was to start the process of privatisation. Gdynia was the first to move, and Gdańsk has only, in late 1997, now reached the private sector purchased by a combination of a Polish steel exporting company and a west European forwarding company. None of the other three Hartwig companies has progressed towards the private market at all.

The main shareholder in Hartwig Gdynia is the Polish Bank for the Development of Exports (Bank Rozwoju Eksportu), the third biggest bank in Poland, which has a 75% stake in the company. The remainder is owned 15% by the employees and 10% by the state. The final move to private status occurred on the 1st July, 1995 with the creation of a joint stock company. Hartwig has also expanded its overseas portfolio during the 1990s which now stretches beyond Amerpol in the US to include C. Hartwig Deutschland in Germany and PSA transport in the United Kingdom.

Hartwig has faced increasing competition since the liberalisation of the forwarding marketplace which, of course, presented the company with the opportunities for development that have taken place. Four main types of competition can be identified :

(1) The totally private sector, set up commonly by ex Hartwig employees who can use their existing contacts to help them progress and survive in the market. The Polish Association of Freight Forwarders, of which Hartwig is a member, lists over 90 in the Gdynia area alone although many are very small and frequently less than three employees in size.

(2) Companies which were and still are, state owned. These operators tend to be very diversified in their specialisms emerging for example, from Polish Ocean Lines, PZM, MAG and the old Foreign Trade Organisations and concentrating largely upon related work.

(3) Totally foreign based companies including organisations such as Scansped of Sweden. These companies numbered few in 1997 but their international status poses a great threat to the established Polish forwarders and the prediction is for considerably more competition in the future.

(4) Completely new individuals to the profession - of which there are very few.

Undoubtedly the level of competition has increased dramatically from the days of the old regime and the most significant of these competitors are often ex-Hartwig employees or sections of other ex-state shipping industries that have emerged during the liberalised phase.

The market

As the market has become deregulated and as the shipping industry as a whole has begun the slow process of restructuring, the client base for the forwarding industry has changed dramatically. Under the old system, the clients were easy to identify, rarely changed and were allocated to each Hartwig company. In effect they constituted the twenty Foreign Trade Organisations (FTO) that were operated by the state to organise the import, export and trade finance for all commodities traded between Poland and the outside world. In a similar style to all the CMEA countries, these FTOs were state owned and operated, providing a monopoly service that facilitated the control of trade and, most importantly, that of hard currency movements. Hartwig, as the state forwarding company, benefited from this close relationship but upon liberalisation of the economy, the role of the FTOs disappeared as well, with the introduction of freedom for any individual or organisation to trade internationally. Hartwig's customer base thus disappeared alongside the FTOs and a whole new client structure has had to be created.

Hartwig has been successful in this process and moved into new commodities, new modes and a new client base. The twenty FTOs have been replaced by a substantially increased number of clients but the quantity of business carried out with each has declined to an even greater extent, resulting in a reduced turnover of volume from the 1980s. Some truck freighting is now organised, but effectively no air freight and the business remains, as in the past, dominated by container sea freight - a result of Gdynia's legacy of this type of activity as a port. The main international destinations dealt with are the whole of the European short sea market including especially the United Kingdom, the USA/Canada and the Far East. 1995 turnover, the last figures available, reached some 45000 TEU and 1m tonnes of cargo. Hartwig Gdynia's pretensions to a widespread new market base are thus limited so far - but future ambitions include a vision of Gdynia as an expanding transit base for trade to and from the Baltic States, Belarus, the Kaliningrad enclave (Russia) and the Ukraine.

Some bulk trading has been taken on including quantities of grain, steel, chemicals, agricultural commodities (especially soya), bulk sugar and project cargoes. These represent the traditional bulk commodities of Gdynia and Gdańsk with the exception of the coal and oil trades which tend to remain with the forwarders that emerged from the shipping companies that dominated these trades.

In addition to the overseas activities noted earlier in the United Kingdom, Germany and the USA, Hartwig Gdynia has also a number of domestic activities spread around Poland. These include the ownership and operation of C. Hartwig Transport Services - an international trucking company with 35 vehicles which operates independently of the parent company and is only sometimes used for Hartwig Gdynia's trucking needs; a warehouse in Gdynia which has been recently modernised; another in Poznań with some 8000 square metres of storage, located reasonably close to the German border and thus ideally suited for the development of transit traffic to and from the west; and a series of share ownerships in over twenty companies around Poland which have been inherited in lieu of debt payments over the years and which are located in widely diversified activities. The future of these stakes was under close review in late 1997. Hartwig also has offices located in both Gdańsk and Gdynia ports and more significantly, representatives of the company in Katowice and Warsaw in Poland, Budapest (Hungary) and Riga (Latvia) indicating its desire and plans to move beyond its traditional market mode, location and commodities. Perhaps another good indication of the increasing independence and westernisation of the company is that all domestic trucking is now carried out by independent contractors, some 150 of which are placed upon an approved listing.

Company structure

The company has around 330 employees, the majority of which work in the headquarters building in Gdynia. This is a reduction on the total that was employed under the old regime and unfortunately, it has resulted from the loss of many of the more talented and young employees who have frequently gone on to form competitors to Hartwig themselves. Hartwig has adapted its formal structure since privatisation a number of times, the last being in May 1997. Figure 29 gives an indication of the latest position.

Despite the creation of a new marketing and development division in May 1995, there has been little evidence of its work. However, its creation is an indication of the desire of the company to provide a marketing framework for the organisation and to move earlier practices based around sales and undertaken throughout the company, into a structured format and a co-ordinated approach.

Figure 29
C. Hartwig Gdynia - company structure, 1997

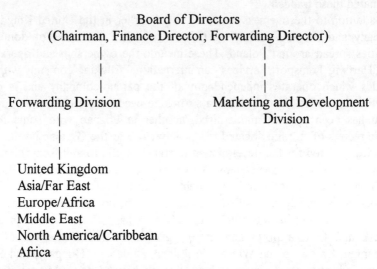

Board of Directors
(Chairman, Finance Director, Forwarding Director)

Forwarding Division   Marketing and Development
                                                    Division

United Kingdom
Asia/Far East
Europe/Africa
Middle East
North America/Caribbean
Africa

Source : C.Hartwig Gdynia, 1997

Company finances reflect the stability of the company and certainly suggest that Hartwig Gdynia will survive the transitional phase in the maritime sector and should move from there to further strengthen its position. The company has been profitable since privatisation and with slow but continuing diversification, it should continue to remain this way.

The strategy for company development of diversification, based around the new company structure adopted in May 1997 intends to continue the infiltration of new markets and includes the development of the marketing process. Achievement of ISO9002 is an early ambition whilst office facilities are being revamped and modern computing facilities have been fully introduced.

Some conclusions

C. Hartwig Gdynia presents some interesting examples of contradiction in the Polish maritime market place and in particular, the survival of an ex-state owned company in a new aggressive market environment - but a company although with clear desires to expand client base, commodities and geographical area, as yet with only limited success. Privatisation and the impact of new private owners and capital have clearly had some effect on both operations and strategy but in contrast, it is interesting to note the limited development of the marketing function after some two years of activity under the new owners. The new company structure, including a dedicated marketing division, should make some difference here.

Hartwig Gdynia contrasts vividly with the inactivity in the private sector of the Szczecin branch where existing and traditional markets and functions remain dominant. The activity within the Gdynia based company should hold them in good stead in the years to come as the competition from other newly emerging forwarding companies becomes more intense and the resulting squeeze on traditional markets becomes that much clearer. The example of the use of a range of private sector truck operators in Polish domestic work, each vetted and chosen for Hartwig's selected list, is a good one for the newly developing forwarding sector and one that others within the marketplace would be sensible to follow. Even their own international trucking company, C. Hartwig Transport Services, has no guarantee of receiving the parent company traffic and in fact, must commonly operate in competition with other services arranged by the parent for international movements.

Future years will reveal the wisdom of the Hartwig Gdynia strategy, but in late 1997 it looks a good pattern for other forwarding companies to attempt to follow.

C. Hartwig Szczecin

Introduction

C. Hartwig Szczecin is one of the longest established international forwarding companies in Poland centred on the region of Western Pomerania - i.e. around the Szczecin area. Its role is one of the traditional freight forwarding company providing facilities for the movement of a large variety of cargoes from bulk loads to small consolidations and with a speciality in heavy lift transport. Container movements, dangerous goods and break-bulk consignments are all catered for. All areas of the world are covered by all modes with a clear and obvious concentration upon Polish sourced goods.

Once the monopoly provider of freight forwarding in the region under state ownership, we shall see how C. Hartwig has had to adapt to the new competitive environment and how far plans for privatisation and restructuring have progressed. Firstly, though, to gain a better understanding of the current situation, we need to examine the company's historical development up to the present day.

Historical development of the company

The company had its origins with a citizen of Poznań - Carl Hartwig - who formed C. Hartwig in 1858 in the city to provide local freight transport services. The company was highly successful, so that by the inter-war period, although now owned by a consortium of banks, it had branches in all major Polish cities and covered the country as well as providing international facilities for freight through a network of overseas correspondents and representatives.

With the return of Szczecin (Stettin in German) in 1945 to Poland from German occupation, a new branch was set up in the city with the name of C. Hartwig Szczecin specialising on marine transport but with interests in the land distribution side. The Communist controlled state took over most of the company during the immediate post-war period although a small proportion remained in private overseas hands. The company then focused upon one geographical area alone - including and concentrating upon Szczecin, Świnoujście and Kołobrzeg - specialising in heavy loads and those with non-standard dimensions. International forwarding activities developed from there on behalf of the state Ministry of Foreign Trade and with a monopoly of activities in both geographical and commercial areas.

Any residual private, overseas ownership was taken over in 1970 and the company - along with the other subsidiaries in Gdynia, Gdańsk, Warsaw and Katowice - became totally state owned, managed and controlled. Each branch was allocated its own speciality with those in Gdynia, Gdańsk and Szczecin designated as the maritime forwarders and those in Katowice and Warsaw designated inland forwarders with their own specific spatial responsibilities. Each was independent of each other, with their own finances and management but each the responsibility of the state. Close co-operation between companies was encouraged in order to ensure a smooth pattern of international forwarding. The existing Foreign Trade Organisations (FTOs) at the time were required under state regulations to use only Hartwig for all international forwarding activities and prescribed detailed procedures concerning the nature of the collaboration and process. The only exceptions to this were a very limited number of bulk commodity shippers who organised their own transport services (e.g. some coal, sulphur and grain) with the specific permission of the Ministry.

With the social, political and economic changes of the late 1980s and 1990s, and the new regulatory framework of 1988 and 1989, C. Hartwig achieved a considerable degree of increased economic, managerial and financial independence that it has retained to today but which also opened up the market to others. Whilst remaining under state ownership in Szczecin - although not in all other branches - the distance between the state and the company has notably increased with the growing anticipation of privatisation.

The company today

The company remains based in Szczecin with outlying offices in Świnoujście and Kołobrzeg. The main functions of the company today have evolved from its history and centre around the storage and transportation of international consignments, the organisation of such facilities for clients in Poland and abroad, customs clearance and formalities, completion of all documentation requirements associated with these activities and all contractual procedures that follow from this as well. The company owns its own warehouse (in Police to the immediate north of Szczecin) of 20000sqm (covered) and 5000sqm (open) storage, a fleet of trucks and is in possession of "Customs Agency No. 34" and as such can declare and clear goods at these locations and at any Polish international border.

All modes of transport are dealt with - although the maritime mode remains the most significant - and interests in the trucking and air side have been developed in recent years since the removal of state controls on the company activities.

The main export cargoes handled centre around coal concentrates, cereals, cement, chemicals, fuels and a wide variety of general cargo including containerised volumes, textile and furniture. Import cargoes include ore, phosphorous carriers, apatites, magnetites, bauxites, coke and general cargo of a variety of types. Transit cargo, in particular has grown and now includes regular shipments to and from the Ukraine, Latvia, Russia, the Czech Republic, Slovakia and Germany. It is notable that the dominant commodities in import, export and transit trades are heavy industrial products. Finally, the company is beginning to specialise in heavy-lift and awkward, non-standard loads in the Szczecin region, including recent deliveries to local fertiliser and chemical companies and timber processors.

The company currently employs around 250 staff which reflects a massive reduction in numbers from the peak of around 530 in the early 1970s - when it had a monopoly on all forwarding in the region across as far as and including Kołobrzeg. This encompassed all the Oder ports - Szczecin, Świnoujście, Stepnica and Police in particular - in addition. The reason for the decline in staff, which incidentally has been achieved without any compulsory redundancies, is the surge in competition that followed the deregulation of the forwarding market so that from a position of monopoly, C. Hartwig now faces competition from 39 other forwarding companies in Szczecin alone.

The company is structured internally rather curiously, with eight departments, some service based (e.g. ferries), some trade direction based (e.g. import or export), some trade based (e.g. chemicals) and some seemingly haphazardly based (e.g. transit and groupage). Office departments also exist for administration, accounting and finance.

Turnover of the company has increased in new złoty terms from a figure of 200 million in 1993, to 250 million in 1994 and 300 million in 1995. Tonnage handled has gone from 3.98m tonnes in 1992, to 3.86m tonnes in 1993, 4.64m tonnes in 1994 and 5.01m tonnes in 1995. This rise in turnover and tonnage may seem curious in the light of the earlier comments about the new competition that has arisen but needs to be seen in the light of a fall in tonnage from 12.0m tonnes in the 1970s. What is also apparent is that the chronic overmanning of the old regime's days has had to be tackled (through staff reductions) and the profit margin to be made on this recently increased tonnage and turnover has substantially reduced in the new competitive environment. The company remains profitable and has few if any debts but this situation will remain difficult to sustain with the current workforce level and the increasing competition.

Some 90% of the turnover is raised from marine activities and the 4000 clients that the company now serves, with the vast majority of the rest road and storage based - a legacy from the state's dominant days. This is not necessarily a very good sign as modal choice within Poland is actively moving towards the trucking mode away from sea and rail transport wherever possible typified by the almost complete loss of Szczecin's general cargo trade from the port to trucking across Europe and to competing ports in Germany in particular. The size of client base is impressive but reflects a large number of small players in a market once dominated by a very small number of state industries. Administration costs, as a result, have climbed and the logistical complications of all this are substantial to a company, perhaps not well prepared for the changes that have occurred.

Marketing is one aspect of the company that is supposed to have been developed and its significant role for the future recognised. However, closer inspection reveals the use of a very limited number of traditional approaches including a restricted number of trade press advertisements, a limited number of "glossy publications", appearance at trade fairs and some telephone sales. Despite the existence of a marketing leader in the company, no-one actually concentrates on marketing itself despite the huge growth in competition and the recognised decline in status from the monopolistic days of the 1980s and before. According to the senior management, marketing efforts are expected of all staff, but in practice very little is actually done about it as an issue.

The company, as with all the Hartwig companies, is a member of the Polish International Freight Forwarders Association which lobbies on behalf of the industry and has done so since its formation in 1993.

Privatisation

The first indications that the Szcecin branch of C. Hartwig should be privatised by the state owners emerged in December 1994 when the company submitted a request and plan to the then Ministry of International Economic Co-operation. Progress since then has been very slow, although other branches, notably those in Gdynia and Gdańsk, have achieved private status by 1996 - these latter two companies were sold off for differing reasons and in different circumstances in that the former was suffering from substantial financial problems and the latter was bought by a combination of Polish and German interests. It is anticipated, at least by the company, that full privatisation will be completed during 1997, and the earliest date being discussed was March 1997 although outside commentators felt that this was considerably optimistic and in fact by July 1997, no progress had been made. An original date for transfer was December 1996 but the recent changes in the Treasury structure and organisation led to this being delayed. Privatisation is seen as a most important phase in the company's development as remaining a state owned and managed company results in high levels of taxation, greater wage controls and poorer image in a market place increasingly recognising the role of this latter factor.

The most recent plan is for the existing C. Hartwig Szczecin organisation to be liquidated and a new company - C. Hartwig International Forwarders - created with the notable omission of the Szczecin reference implying a spread of activities and geographical influence. This would be owned largely by the current employees with a small part available to pensioners of the company. The distribution of shares would be made on the basis of position in the company, length of service and income in that order of importance, commencing with position. Shares would have to be purchased and the aim would be that the full cost of these shares would be spread over a number of years so that they could be affordable to anyone in the company who would wish to purchase them . The debt would be payable to the state over an agreed length of time and upon successful completion, the company would be fully privatised.

One alternative approach to privatisation was rejected at an early stage, and that was using investment from overseas in a way similar to the Gdańsk branch. Fear of losing control of the business and the immediate danger of job losses were enough to encourage the company to explore the employee buy-out approach that has been adopted. Foreign competition in the market place of forwarding has already raised its head noticeably in the Szczecin region including such notable companies as Danzas from Switzerland.

Discussion

C. Hartwig Szczecin displays many of the problems facing the state maritime sector as it has to come to grips with the changes taking place in the Polish economy as a whole and as it attempts to move from public ownership, at least partially into private hands. For the sake of convenience and interpretation we can divide the problems which exist and the issues that will need to be dealt with into a number of specific categories.

(1) Market share - C. Hartwig Szczecin has already experienced a substantial drop in the market share that it enjoys in the Szczecin region and in particular, the quantity of business that it receives from the sizeable client base that it has retained. In fact this client base has actually expanded since the days of monopoly and directed traffic as the market has changed and the state no longer dominates the suppliers of shipments but the unfortunate consequence of all this is that the overall administrative burden is considerably higher and the profit to be made from each of the services provided is, in fact considerably less than it was. Fragmentation is the order of the day with considerably more clients to satisfy and with which to keep in close contact.

(2) Competition - the effects on market share are largely the result of competition, which did not realistically exist before the changes of the late 1980s when the company concentrated on a majority of the commodities moving through the ports of the region leaving only a minority of specialised products to be organised by the shippers themselves. The result, therefore was a small number of state run clients with predictable and guaranteed shipments and little if any demand for high levels of service within a competitive framework. All that has changed and C. Hartwig now finds itself just one of many forwarders in the region attempting to retain, and hopefully increase market share. In fact the aggressive nature of the new entrants into this market place has meant that the company has lost trade and now faces an uncertain future. The idea that the years of experience of the company would hold it in good stead when the competition developed, may in fact have been wrong and that the association of the company with the old regime and its characteristics may now act as a drag on new developments, as attitudes are difficult to alter within the company and reputation difficult to change without.

(3) Trades - C. Hartwig Szczecin remains fixed on the old trades that characterised its activities in the post-war period up to the time of change in the Polish economy, dominated by heavy industry and chemicals, ores, grain and coal in particular. These industries are in relative decline in the new Poland where consumer markets dominated by hi-tech and light goods are the growth areas and C. Hartwig must be careful that it does not decline with them. In a similar fashion it remains dominated by the maritime marketplace from which 90% of turnover comes. In the current climate of modal transfer from sea to truck wherever this is feasible and the consequent decline in the use of Szczecin/Świnoujście as a major Polish port in comparison with

Hamburg, Bremerhaven and even Rotterdam and Antwerp to the west of Poland, Hartwig's market share will continue to decline.

(4) Diversification - despite these quite clear problems, the company has done nothing to diversify from its traditional base and its traditional market region of the north west of Poland and Szczecin/Świnoujście port in particular. This is in stark contrast to many new competitors in the region who have taken on the role of forwarder, broker, charterer, large-scale warehouse operator, consultant, transport operator and so on. Even previous allies in C. Hartwig Gdynia for example, have entered new markets and shown how new regions of Poland can be invaded and won. The Gdynia branch, now privatised, has offices campaigning for business, not only in Gdynia but also in Warsaw, Katowice and neighbouring Gdańsk, all beyond the original definition of their home territory and in direct competition with other Hartwig companies. The Szczecin company remains constrained to its original territory and offices (Szczecin, Świnoujście and Kołobrzeg) with clear implications for the future of the company and its ability to develop and increase market share and a diversified client and product range. The company had considered the benefits that might emerge from spatial diversification but had rejected it as a policy as it might lead to the neglect of local and established clients who had been very valuable over many years and the thinning of coverage over a wider geographical area with the resultant loss of image and reputation. One attitude that seems to permeate the company was that no loss had ever been made, consequently was there really a true need to diversify anyway?

(5) Physical and staffing constraints - the company remains dominated by the staff who have remained from the days before economic, social and political change and by its own admission this is increasingly those who cannot move on or who are too old to move on as the young and vibrant forwarders of the future choose to leave and set up independently, move to new foreign invaders or never join the company in the first place. Little more needs to be said other than the fact that some of the highest ranking staff in the company have been with Hartwig since the early 1950s. The structure of the company remains state influenced and largely chaotic with departments failing to reflect the market trends and with little rationale for their continued existence. Physical equipment, buildings, furniture and decor are also less than inspiring although plans are afoot to move to new premises (to reduce costs given the reduction in staff and, therefore the lower need for space) when privatisation takes place.

Some conclusions

Overall, C. Hartwig Szczecin presents what might be considered a typically old style reaction to the changes that have taken place in the Polish maritime sector, if such a type of reaction is identifiable anywhere. Much of this reaction is very understandable but it has to be questioned whether the company has realistic hopes of thriving - or even surviving - in the new forwarding environment of Poland dominated by small private companies needing little capital investment, and whom have often gained their experience and contacts from time spent previously with a Hartwig company, or larger and more resourceful overseas companies with substantial back-up, widespread experience of western markets and extensive marketing skills.

Baltona S.A. Przedsiębiorstwo Handlu Zagranicznego

Introduction

Baltona S.A. is the previously state owned company that provided, amongst other services, ship supplies to both domestically flagged and foreign flagged vessels entering and leaving Polish ports. In recent years, as we shall see, Baltona has become rather more diverse the markets and products that it sells and as such has become notably orientated. However, as a product of the state maritime sector under es, it remains of some significance to this work, albeit as a fringe me the companies that have been assessed.

Development and current status

Baltona was originally established as a private joint stock compa on the 3rd September 1946 to carry out shipchandling activities within the Polish state. As a consequence of the nationalisation of the Polish economy in 1949, following the rise of Communism and the increasing influence of the neighbouring Soviet Union, the company was compulsorily liquidated and replaced by the state owned Foreign Trade Enterprise, Baltona.

Baltona expanded into other trading areas over the coming years including the supply of duty free zones, the provision of commodities for embassies, border crossing sales and the sale of goods for hard currency to Polish seafarers. In 1970, Baltona took over trading activities from a number of other state enterprises including providing catering services for the state carrier LOT Polish airlines and providing other services for exhibitions and trade fairs abroad.

On January 2nd 1984, the status of the company changed once again, formed into a wholly state owned joint stock company. Baltona then entered the retail sector and was allowed to sell imported goods to the general public for hard currency. This ceased in 1991 with the abolition of hard currency goods sales following the political, social and economic changes of the period.

Currently, Baltona has been substantially restructured but with only very long term and rather unclear proposals for final and full privatisation in the future. Figure 30 gives an indication of the current owners which is a very diverse set and yet at the same time dominated by a mix of banks, LOT Polish Airlines, Polska Żegluga Morska (PZM), the Ministry in Warsaw and the majority shareholder, a commercial bank in Luxembourg. Eventually this will undoubtedly include the transfer of all the company's assets to the private sector, but due to its relatively untroubled existence and its small political significance, it may not be for some time.

Figure 30
Significant/major shareholders in Baltona - 1997

Shareholder	Shares (number)
C. Hartwig Gdynia	2
C. Hartwig Warsaw	2
Polfracht	2
Central state Ministry	4790
LOT Polish Airlines	2276
PZM	70
Bank Polska Kasa Opieki S.A. Warsaw	1036
Pekpol Import/export	89
Polish Ocean Lines	10
Polfracht	2
Port Authority of Szczecin-Świnoujście	14
Polska Żegluga Bałtycka	4
Directors of the company	2 each
Grupa Inwestycyjna NYWIG S.A. Warsaw	9262
(Representatives of a commercial bank in Luxembourg - this figure constitutes 51% of the Company share ownership)	
Other shareholders	276

Source: Baltona PHZ, 1997

The company is currently managed by a President and General Director, a Vice President and Commercial Director, and a Director of Management and Finance from offices currently being redeveloped in the suburbs of Gdynia.

The main activities

Baltona's current main activities can be divided up into the following categories.

(1) Retail trading. Baltona has 34 retail shops in Poland located either in major airports - Okęcie (Warsaw) in particular - in city centres in Warsaw, Gdynia, Gdańsk etc., or at border crossings on highways. Three main types of commodity are available through these outlets - food, beverages, alcohol and cigarettes; cosmetics and clothing; and technical products including audio, video and household equipment.

Sales through the retail side of the trade now amount to around 40% of the total turnover and this is now the main sector of the business.

(2) Duty free sales. Baltona's duty free operations include sales in two shops at Warsaw International Airport (Okęcie) and also the sale of goods to foreign ships entering Polish waters and calling at Polish seaports.

This latter activity is decreasing in significance to the company as a whole as it adapts to the changing economic environment of Poland in the 1990s and the changes occurring in transport modal demand from ship to truck and air. However, Baltona retains around a 40% market share of all duty free goods largely through its outlets at Warsaw Airport. New airport shops are planned for Gdańsk, Wrocław, Kraków and Katowice Airports with some 50% of all sales represented by domestic and imported alcohol and beer. Cigarettes make up another 22-25% of sales. Overall this sector represents the biggest income for Baltona.

(3) Wholesale services. Wholesale services mainly concentrate upon the provision of alcoholic beverages to a limited number of customers. In total they constitute some 10% of the company's turnover.

(4) Shipchandling. Ship supply has been Baltona's core business since the foundation of the company and it remains a significant part of the business. Some US$15 million of business was conducted by Baltona in 1996 in the ship chandling field. Baltona was an early member of the International Ship Suppliers Association (ISSA) an organisation that represents some 1800 shipchandlers from all over the world. Of the 30 Polish shipchandling companies, only four (including Baltona) are members of the ISSA and thus

can meet its exacting standards - the others are POL-Supply, an offshoot of Polish Ocean Lines, Neptun Ship Service (both based in Gdynia) and Handloship (based in Szczecin) with two others - Sea Commerce (Gdynia) and Mr Mate (Szczecin) who are applying for membership.

Baltona remains the biggest shipchandler in Poland even though it no longer enjoys the monopoly of the Communist days, and operates in all the four international Polish ports of Gdańsk, Gdynia, Szczecin and Świnoujście. It has presided over the Polish Ship Supplier Association that was formed on 1st June 1995 as the number of companies in the market grew as a response to liberalisation within the industry.

(5) Export. Baltona also has small interests in the export of light industrial and food products to Europe and overseas.

In addition, since September 1996, Baltona has also operated a deposit store at the Świnoujście ferry terminal for containers and semi-trailers as well as a bonded warehouse and a number of storage facilities. The company offers services for bonding, customs clearance and the storage, handling and carriage of goods including those that are refrigerated. A new subsidiary company - Baltona Depo Ltd. - has been set up to provide the customs agency services.

A major development is the opening of a warehouse, offices and retail facilities in Klaipeda (Lithuania) and then from there on into the other Baltic States and the Former Soviet Union. The major problem identified with these developments is that of finance and in particular the reliability of payments from an unstable economic framework. A new company wholly owned by the Baltona parent has been established to operate this concern - Baltona Klaipeda.

To manage all these activities the company has head offices in Gdynia and branch offices and warehouses in Gdańsk, Warsaw, Katowice, Szczecin and Świnoujście. Total employees at the 1st July, 1997 was 315 which represents some 200-250 less than in the time before the changes of the late 1980s.

Discussion

This short review of the activities of Baltona provides some further insights into the adaptation process occurring within the Polish maritime sector. In particular, it reveals the development of diversification that is now being encouraged throughout most of the industry and which most of those active within the sector are now following. Baltona - once almost exclusively a shipchandling enterprise, now receives most of its income from other sectors which is also where most of its developments now occur in particular, those relating to duty-free sales. Shipping related activities are now undoubtedly second to those in Warsaw Airport and in the future this is likely to be exacerbated as a trend as new facilities are opened at Gdańsk and Kraków and other international airports.

However, Baltona continues to act as the most important ship chandlers in Poland despite the rise of alternative competitors in both Szczecin and Gdynia. The competition is not as fierce as in the broking or agency sectors, for example, largely because of the nature of the business itself but the development of something like 35 alternative ship suppliers has presented the company with a series of real and difficult issues that have had to be faced.

Baltona has adapted well, diversifying their activities as we have seen but into areas that provide advantages of synergy. They have also learned to work with their competitors through the formation of the Polish Ship Suppliers Association of which they remain the dominant member. In this way it can help to direct the industry and thus retain an important position within the market place.

Baltona has undoubtedly suffered as a result of the decline in the Polish economy that had occurred up to 1995 and which by 1997 was only just being reversed, resulting in a reduced level of shipping activity and thus shipping needs. The loss of its monopoly position was also clearly important and the impact upon employment within the company is apparent.

Baltona's new ownership structure also deserves comment as it reflects a wide variety of trends that have been seen to be taking place within the maritime sector as a whole. The wide number of investors is notable, although they are dominated by a few major owners. The majority share owner is located in Luxembourg and represented in Poland by the company NYWIG of Warsaw thus placing control of the company abroad with substantial tax and other fiscal advantages. The Ministry retains a large shareholding (although for how long remains unclear) whilst other significant (and small) shareholdings can be found with many related industries, many of which are still largely state owned or have previous state interests. These include LOT Polish Airlines, Polish Ocean Lines, PZM, PZB and the Port of Szczecin-Świnoujście. Significantly, the Board of Directors also own parts of the company reflecting the slowly increasing diversification of ownership amongst other interests.

Baltona remains a small player in the maritime ancillary sector, but one that displays many of the characteristics occurring in the development of the industry and as such, it presents an interesting case for further analysis.

Conclusions

Introduction

This section attempts to bring together a number of themes which emerge from the earlier discussion and which in terms of this text attempts to address the issues emanating from the effects of commercialisation and privatisation in the Polish maritime industries. It would be impossible to attempt to cover all the issues that have emerged but a large number of the major and most interesting developments have become apparent and are indicated here.

In summary, the major conclusions can be indicated as follows:

(1) The industry, from all directions and including all players, has faced a traumatic time since the late 1980s when the first deregulation and liberalisation occurred and the monopoly within the maritime market of all services and providers was broken. No part of the industry has remained unaffected and this is clearly reflected in the discussion in this text ranging from the development of new ferry competitors operating into and out of Gdynia (and based in Sweden), through the huge influx and development of forwarders, agents and brokers largely in the private sector and constituting very small companies in general, to the restructuring of the ports sector and the new role to be played by the private companies supplying operational services to the market. There are a whole host of new companies, privatised old state companies, reformed state companies and residual state companies who have diversified their location of activity and their nature of work. There are so many examples it is difficult to pick one out - but perhaps the newly restructured Polfracht, located in new offices in Gdynia, providing western

style services to a broad range of the market - yet still state owned, sums up the continuing flexible situation.

(2) There is quite clearly within this highly mobile market place, a distinct difference between those companies that have wholeheartedly taken on board the new environment and those that linger rather more in the past. Even the latter have to face the new competitive environment but many have done little more than to learn some new marketing language and to revise their marketing literature. These companies are typified by Morska Agencja Szczecin, who unlike their namesakes in Gdynia and Gdańsk, remain state owned with plans but few prospects for an early transfer to the private sector. Their market is limited in scope and geographical area, their physical presence typical of the old system and their attitude to change unpromising. It is difficult to see how, over the long term, they can survive.

Similar to this is the position within the ports sector, where active attempts are being made to adapt to the new structural changes of ownership being forced upon the main international players - Gdańsk, Gdynia and Szczecin/Świnoućjcie - but where the tangible effects of change so far are few. Port Authorities remain locked in the attitudes of the past and, effectively will remain in state hands for years to come - contrasting with the port operations sector which is well on the way to restructuring and full privatisation. The latter also, are often formed from employee buyouts and as such may not be as dynamic as the new companies in the maritime sector overall, formed from ex-employees moving from state industries to be independent, or new players altogether that are entering the ancillaries sector in particular. In some cases there was also evidence of the Port Authorities continuing to support these new operational companies with favourable rates and conditions. True privatisation has some way to move yet before it is a reality.

(3) The situation within the shipping companies is rather more interesting. Here, where the financial problems inherited from the old regime were perhaps more substantial and where the capital investment needed is undoubtedly sizeable (and at the same time unavailable), the problems faced upon transition were almost insurmountable. Shipping being what it is however, has created a new situation of intense commercialism that the Polish market has grasped fully, and despite continued state involvement at all levels and to a substantial degree, each of the companies is moving forwards in restructuring in anticipation of complete and full privatisation. The complexity of company ownership and involvement has now become severe however, as a result of the need to avoid taxation, prevent seizure of assets and as the natural entrepreneurial spirit of Polish shipping interests raises its head. Thus

Polish Ocean Lines presents a fascinating case study of the adaptation of the industry so far - restructured yet not truly privatised; commercialised with no ships operated by the parent company; with subsidiaries, in legal terms private but owned ultimately by the state; with massive debts and no real prospect of insolvency; with plans for entering new markets around the world with new ships; with few Polish flagged vessels any more and "daughter" companies stretching across the world protecting assets and effectively moving the once domestic industry into the international shipping environment. It is in the shipping sector that the most interesting developments are still to come. They were (and to some extent still are) state representatives and their full privatisation is thus hindered by a political need to retain them within the Polish national economy; at the same time their is insufficient interest or money within the Polish economy to retain them in a privatised form. The result is the current restructuring in Polish Ocean Lines (and incidentally, PZM) necessary for survival, with a gloss of Polish ownership placed over the transfer of assets and control abroad.

(4) All industrial players have diversified into related areas and commonly beyond their historically defined geographical areas. Thus POL owns ferries, Polsteam Tankers operate vessels that never return to Poland, the Port Authorities have created Duty Free Zones, Polfracht have become property developers and so on. There has become a need to diversify to survive matched by an opportunity to do so in the newly deregulated market. Further diversification is expected as the years pass by. The one notable exception here is C. Hartwig of Szczecin who remain largely constrained to their old role and location - part of which is undoubtedly a function of the nature of the company leadership and the need for new blood.

(5) All the industries contacted, including those not included in detail in this text, have divested jobs. A requirement of the deregulation and restructuring process has been the shrinking of the workforce usually accomplished by voluntary means. One problem resulting from this has been that those individuals most talented have tended to be those that have departed first (commonly to form their own companies in the private sector), leaving behind the oldest and least able to adapt to the new environment. Those companies restructuring and privatising earliest - or at least moving as closely as possible to a private sector structure - have fared the best here as they have been able to retain their better workers in a more dynamic market with greater and more immediate rewards (and risks). POL Levant is a good example of this where an early decision was taken to restructure to avoid the loss of key personnel.

175

(6) There is clearly a new attitude towards activities within the maritime sector in Poland but one which is confined to the younger element of the industry and which recognises the need to adapt diversify and change. This is most apparent in the ancillary sector where the greatest amount of new private activity is taking place and least evident in the ports sector where it is fair to conclude that the level of immediate competition is at its lowest level. The ship operators lie somewhere in between partly facing intense international competition but also receiving political protection from the worst effects of deregulation and privatisation.

(7) One thread running through the industry as a whole is the benefit it undoubtedly still feels from its exposure to international competition in the past. This has provided the impetus for change in the shipping and ports sector and the experience with which to survive in a particularly fierce commercial sector. Once again, the ports sector has least benefited from this exposure, being able to rely on a guaranteed, monopoly market far more than the shipping interests and the Port Authority attitudes analysed in this text clearly reflect this.

(8) There is a real fear of foreign invasion in all sectors. Even the ports sector now recognises the dangers inherent in the role of Hamburg, Rotterdam and other north western European ports in taking domestic and transit trade. The shipping companies expressed considerable agitation at the fiercely competitive attitude of Maersk Line which now provides container feeder services from Gdynia and the ferry operators fears expressed at the expansion of Lion Ferry operated and owned by Stena Line of Sweden. There was a clear mismatch between the expressed favour of a free market in the industry, and the need to protect Polish shipping interests against unfair foreign commercial practices.

The Polish shipping industry is not lacking in advantages particularly in comparison with the maritime sectors in many other of the ex state owned industries of the former East Europe. It has an international reputation of some standing and a tradition in the shipping sector which is important and well known. In terms of the ports sector, Poland's location is in some ways advantageous as the country lies midway between the thriving economies of Scandinavia and the developing economies of the Middle East. The ancillary sector is relatively developed and entry is easy for newcomers.

However at the same time there are obvious disadvantages. Much of the industry's equipment in ports and in the form of vessels is old and needs renewing. Only limited progress has been made here - e.g. "Boomerang" and the "Polonia" - and the linked inland transport services including railways and

176

roads are only slowly catching up. Inland waterways remain underused and inadequate. Meanwhile there remains considerable evidence of the old guard still at the helm of much of the industry with all the attitudes and skills of the old regime and finding it very difficult to adapt and change, even if they wish to. Clear evidence of this latter problem comes from the ports and the agency sectors. The environment for the shipping industry within Poland remains monolithic and monopolistic even if the ancillary industries are open to competitive pressure and the shipping sector to pressures from elsewhere including other modes. Entry to the shipping market remains difficult, inhibited by a combination of a shortage of capital, high interest rates and a political environment that remains unencouraging.

On balance, the ancillaries sector - and particularly the broking, agency and forwarding sectors - shows greatest adaptation, with some notable exceptions. Port operating companies also reflect the changes but Port Authorities show little recognition of the need to alter their approach. In terms of ship operation and ownership, the greatest moves have been in the subsidiaries of PZM and POL which are becoming increasingly dynamic and after a shaky start are beginning to make profits. The three residual state owned companies - PZM, PZB and POL reflect rather less appreciation of the recent mood in the economy and industry. There is no doubt that the time approaches for the release of these three into the private sector - and the recent moves in the privatisation of PZB - albeit slowly - may suggest that is about to begin.

Ideas that are beginning to be understood and taken up include the process of technology transfer and the development of 'Special Economic Zones' to encourage and foster the growth of new technologies and new organisational approaches to transport in general. Poland remains far behind in the development and adoption of logistics in industry including the shipping sector and this will require new technology, training and new attitudes.

The shortage of capital is particularly inhibiting in the shipping sector where the process of flagging out has now reached epidemic proportions as acquisition of finance is largely only available from overseas. Harsh taxation regimes on domestic shipping do not help here either. The proliferation of overseas related companies by the shipping sector is a clear result of the financial context for the industry which is only just beginning to change as domestic banks begin to involve themselves in ship finance. The loss of domestically flagged fleet and the emigration of Polish seafarers to jobs elsewhere is a direct result of this.

Finally, the industry overall shows evidence of continuing deliberate staff shedding, spatial and skills expansion into areas previously untouched and a clear need for the sector to divest itself of the predominance of ageing ex-seafarer staff and the expansion of business skilled younger management. The ancillary sector is already doing this spontaneously with the growth of new independent private brokers, agents and forwarders. The more difficult task of encouraging this in the monolithic ship operation and ports sector is still to come.

Overall there is no doubt that the trend and pace of change will continue in the Polish maritime sector. Recent developments in PZB - moving the company towards a privatisation sale - and in the new ports legislation show this to be the case. However, the introduction of deregulation and its effects upon the established industry has been the easy stage. Now comes the time when previously fully state owned industries need to be moved into the marketplace and left totally exposed to the commercial ferocity of the international logistics and shipping sector. Some well known companies may wither and die as a result but there is no realistic alternative to the continuation of the process of separating the industry from the state. The current situation is one dominated by the rather curious condition of commercialisation in the industry whereby the old state monopolies have been exposed to the market, restructured in format but await the final push. This in turn is held up by a political need to retain a major force within the shipping sector and which prevents the investment of large quantities of foreign capital, particularly in the ship operating companies but probably also in the ports sector. Domestically, there is little interest in investment whether by companies or individuals in loss making (or poor profit making) state monoliths. Restructuring into small profit (or loss) making enterprises helps but the final push towards full privatisation will not be helped by the industry's general structure and asset base. The result, particularly in the ship operating sector is a subversive move abroad, financially and operationally, resulting in job losses domestically but a notional Polish retention of control. It is likely that this process will continue. In the ports sector, the state seems to intend to retain a strategic interest, which fits in well with political needs, whilst facilitating some operational private involvement. This may well be the eventual way ahead, but is moving very slowly. In the ancillary sectors we have the greatest progress with foreign investment, private sector growth and large scale full transformation. The coming years hold a great deal of interest for the maritime community of Poland and as such there is no doubt that this book will need revising soon as the effects of the massive social, political and economic changes continue to be felt.

References

(1) Berenyi I. (1996) *Poland. Government and shipping poles apart.* Seatrade Review. July.

(2) Blazyca G. and Rapacki R. (eds) (1991) *Poland into the 1990s.* Pinter Publishers; London.

(3) Breitzmann K.H. (1996) *Market transition and structural changes in shipping and ports of Baltic sea countries.* Institut für Verkehr und Logistik, Universität Rostock.

(4) Breitzmann K.H. (ed) (1994) *Shipping, ports and transport in transition to a market economy.* Institut für Verkehr und Logistik, Universität Rostock.

(5) Business Central Europe (1997) *Slow death.* April.

(6) Clayton R. (1994) Working without Warsaw. *Fairplay,* May 12.

(7) COWIconsult (1995) *Strategic study of ports and maritime transport in the Baltic Sea.* European Union Regional Group on Ports and Maritime Transport in the Baltic Sea (unpublished).

(8) Ernst and Young (1992) *Doing business in Poland.* Warsaw.

(9) EuroAfrica Shipping Lines Co. Ltd. (1996) *Annual Report.*

(10) European Commission (1996) *EU relations with Poland.* Background Report B/10/96.

(11) Fairplay (1996) Breaking up at POL. *Fairplay,* May 9.

(12) Fairplay (1996) Home to roost. Russia's problems are Poland's gain. *Fairplay,* January 25.

(13) Fairplay (1996) Poland. Excess of success. *Fairplay,* May 9.

(14) Fairplay (1996) Poor connections. *Fairplay,* May 9.

(15) Fairplay (1997) Gdynia takeover 'close'. *Fairplay,* February 27.

(16) Financial Times (1996) *Polish promise.* September 13.

(17) Financial Times (1996) *Polish service industries.* October 30.

(18) Financial Times (1997) *Poland.* March 26.

(19) International Freighting Weekly (1995) *Stena steams into Poland.* August 14.

(20) Kierzkowski H., Okolski M. and Wellisz S. (eds) (1993) *Stabilization and structural adjustment in Poland.* Routledge; London.

(21) Ledger G.D. and Roe M.S. (1993) East European shipping and economic change; a conceptual model. *Maritime Policy and Management,* 20, 3, 229-241.

(22) Ledger G.D. and Roe M.S. (1995) Positional change in the Polish liner shipping market: a framework approach. *Maritime Policy and Management,* 22, 4, 295-318.

(23) Ledger G.D. and Roe M.S. (1996) *East European change and shipping policy.* Avebury; Aldershot.

(24) Linde H. and Tang L. (eds) (1991) *Cooperation and competition between east and west in maritime transport.* Papers presented at the Second International Conference on World Liner Shipping, Gdańsk.

(25) Lloyds List (1995) *Agency finding a big demand for Polish crew.* September 5.

(26) Lloyds List (1995) *New common feeder established by port.* September 5.

(27) Lloyds List (1995) *Poland. Special Report.* September 5.

(28) Lloyds List (1995) *Polish crew agents back trade lobby.* November 9.

(29) Lloyds List (1995) *Unity to expand services.* December 18.

(30) Lloyds List (1996) *Fleet remains on path to privatisation.* September 2.

(31) Lloyds List (1996) *POL's debt for equity plan.* February 8.

(32) Lloyds List (1997) *'Boomerang' arrives in the Baltic.* May 25.

(33) Lloyds List (1997) *Europort applies for terminal in Gdańsk.* May 25.

(34) Lloyds List (1997) *Gdańsk free zone proves popular.* July 17.

(35) Lloyds List (1997) *Gdańsk yard sale pending.* October 18.

(36) Lloyds List (1997) *Gdańsk yard wins backing for new vessel.* May 25.

(37) Lloyds List (1997) *Gdynia celebrates in style.* May 29.

(38) Lloyds List (1997) *Gdynia facility.* October 9.

(39) Lloyds List (1997) *Gdynia. Special report.* September 23.

(40) Lloyds List (1997) *IACS suspends Polish Register.* May 20.

(41) Lloyds List (1997) *Leader.* March 8.

(42) Lloyds List (1997) *Mitsui secures contract for five Polish Steamship bulk carriers.* October 16.

(43) Lloyds List (1997) *New look at ferry links with Poland.* May 26.

(44) Lloyds List (1997) *Poland revamps shipping registry.* October 14.

(45) Lloyds List (1997) *Poland. A special report.* September 24.

(46) Lloyds List (1997) *Polish Baltic move nearer to privatisation.* September 24.

(47) Lloyds List (1997) *Polish ferry privatisation.* August 9.

(48) Lloyds List (1997) *Polish ferry traffic up.* October 18.

(49) Lloyds List (1997) *Polish Register gets ultimatum from IACS.* October 17.

(50) Lloyds List (1997) *Polska Żegluga seeks bidders.* January.

(51) Lloyds List (1997) *IACS ponders fate of Polish Register.* October 15.

(52) Lloyds List (1997) *Major port and yards changes spur maritime sector debate.* May 29.

(53) Lloyds Ship Manager (1992) *Poland. Special Report.* August.

(54) Lloyds Ship Manager (1995) *Poland.* August.

(55) Maritime Institute of Gdańsk (1996) *Maritime economy. Short statistic review.* Instytutu Morskiego, Gdańsk.

(56) Misztal K. (ed.) (1997) *Economic reforms. The maritime transport sector in Poland and Germany.* Institute of Maritime Transport and Seaborne Trade, University of Gdańsk and Institute of Transport and Logistics, University of Rostock.

(57) Pawlowski M. (1992) Polish merchant fleet: will it sink or swim? *Rzeczpospolita.* July 7.

(58) Polish Maritime Review (1997) *Pomerania.* June. p 14.

(59) Polish Maritime Review (1997) *The first fast ferry for Polish operator.* June. pp 29-30.

(60) Polish Maritime Review (1997) *Unity Line.* June.

(61) Polish ports handbooks. (1994 - 1997) Link Szczecin. (Annual).

(62) Polish Shipbrokers Association (1996) *Agency fees in Polish sea ports.*

(63) Polska Żegluga Bałtycka (1996) *Polferries - 20 years.* PZB, Kołobrzeg.

(64) Port Development International (1996) *Baltic bridge.* June.

(65) Port Development International (1996) *Fast forward (C. Hartwig).* June.

(66) Port Gdynia (1996) *Handbook.*

(67) Poznanski K.Z. (1992) Privatisation of the Polish economy: problems of transition. *Soviet Studies,* 44, 4, 641-664.

(68) Roe M.S. (ed.) (1997) *Developments in the Baltic maritime marketplace.* Ashgate; Aldershot.

(69) Roe M.S. (ed.) (1997) *Shipping in the Baltic region.* Avebury; Aldershot.

(70) Rydzkowski W. and Wojewodzka-Krol K. (1996) *Selected issues in Poland's transport policy in the 1990s.* Paper presented at PTRC Summer Annual Meeting.

(71) Sachs J. (1993) *Poland's jump to the market economy.* The MIT Press; Cambridge, Mass.

(72) Seatrade Review (1996) *Slow progress on Act of Seaports bill.* July.

(73) Seatrade Review (1996) *Well stocked yards but no projects.* July.

(74) Spon N. de (1995) World in focus. Poland. *Fairplay*, May 11.

(75) Szczecin - Świnoujście Port Authority (1996) *Port handbook*

(76) The Independent (1996) *Chirac wants Poland in EU by 2000.* September 13.

(77) University of Gdańsk (1988) *Maritime transport in Belgium and Poland.* Maritime Transport Economics Institiute, University of Gdańsk and RUCA, State University Center Antwerp, Department of Transport Economics.

(78) University of Gdańsk (1990) *Maritime transport in Belgium and Poland; A state of the art.* Institute of Maritime Transport and Seaborne Trade.

(79) University of Gdańsk (1991) *Shipping and ports in the national economy.* Maritime Transport Economics Institute, University of Gdańsk.

(80) Zurek J. (ed.) (1997) *Maritime transport and its role in the national economy.* Institute of Maritime Transport and Seaborne Trade, University of Gdańsk and Institute of Marine Studies, University of Plymouth.

Sources

A large number of individuals and organisations have contributed to the research underlying this text. The following list attempts to give an indication of those contacted with apologies to any individuals who may be inadvertantly missed out.

C. Hartwig Gdynia	Zbigniew Potrykus, Procurator Marek Staszkiewicz, Deputy Director Marketing and Development Krzysztof Tyc, Director Marketing and Development
Polfracht, Gdynia	Wiesław Oriol, Managing Director Sławomir Pietrzak, Marketing Manager Jarosław Kubiczek, Chartering Consultant
MAS, Szczecin	Stanisław Borowicz, General Manager Janusz Piersiński, Agency Department
C. Hartwig, Szczecin	Jerzy Wójtowicz, Forwarding Director Juliusz Stępien, General Director Elźbieta Czaińska, Shipping Department Manager
Baltona FTC	Jolanta Philip, Marketing Department

MAG, Gdynia	Zygmunt Śmigielski, Managing Director Krzysztof Laskowski, Chairman
PZB, Kołobrzeg	Leszek Szymaski, Shipping Director
EuroAfrica Shipping Lines, Szczecin	Adolph Wysocki, Deputy Managing Director Leszek Plewiński, Marine Superintendent
Polsteam Tankers Ltd, Gdynia	Maciej Liszko, Manager Technical Department Leskadia Drozdowska, Finance Department Manager
PZM, Szczecin	Janusz Ziomek, Assistant General Director
University of Gdańsk, Sopot	Włodzimierz Rydzkowski, Professor of Transportation Janusz Zurek, Professor of Maritime Economics Krystyna Wojewódzka-Król, Professor of Logistics
POL Levant, Gdynia	Andrzej Osiecimski, Managing Director
Ministry of Transport and Shipping, Warsaw	Krzysztof Dąbrowski, Adviser Albert Borowski, Deputy Director
Port Gdynia	Jan Lewko, Marketing Manager
Port Authority of Gdańsk	Krzysztof Gromadowski, Deputy Commercial Director
Zarząd Portu Szczecin-Świnoujście	Zygfryd Zelman, Marketing and Development Director Bolesław Kułak, Director of Economics and Finance
Gdynia-America Shipping Lines (London) Limited	Wojciech Kossack Managing Director